GONDA BETRIX

GONDA BETRIX

Jumping to Success

Gonda Betrix
with
Julia Attwood-Wheeler

SOUTHERN
BOOK PUBLISHERS

To my parents and to my husband, Des.

ISBN 1 86812 219 0

First edition, first impression 1991

Published by
Southern Book Publishers (Pty) Ltd
PO Box 3103
Halfway House 1685

Cover design by Michael Barnett
Illustrations by Gary Werth
Set in 11 on 12 pt Hanover
by Unifoto (Pty) Ltd, Cape Town
Printed and bound by National Book Printers, Cape

Contents

Foreword
Acknowledgements
Introduction
1. Early years 1
2. Oorskiet and Gunga Din 7
3. England 9
4. Parting with Oorskiet 14
5. Eldorado and Ratification 16
6. My Marriage 24
7. Honey Girl 27
8. Country Cottage and Isis Bridge 35
9. Flaunt and Watchfire 40
10. Training showjumpers 53
    Choosing a potential show-jumper 53
    Training the ex-racehorse 57
    Bringing the rested horse into work 59
    The first three months 60
    The next three months 62
    D Grade 68
    C Grade 70
    B Grade 76
    A Grade 80
11. Working and riding the horse 85
    Work routine 85
12. A word from the vet 89
    Buyer beware! 91
    Lameness affecting show-jumpers 92
    Back problems 102
    Common problems 105
    Summary 106
13. Shoeing the showjumper 109
    The horse as an individual 109
    The objective of shoeing 110
    The foot in motion 110
    The ideal foot 110
    Specifics of South African showjumping 111
    External factors that affect the hoof 113
    Factors specific to each individual horse 115
    Use of the forge 116
    Common problems and corrective action 119
    Other problems 128
14. Feeding the showjumper 129
15. Travelling the horse 131
    Loading 132
    Air travel 133
16. A brief word about riding 135

FOREWORD

I first visited South Africa in 1957, having been invited to open a show and to compete on a horse owned by a dear friend of mine, Bob Grayston.

The horse was Guardsman, and it soon became clear that he was feeling the effects of a hard season in Europe, so we decided to rest him.

This left me without a mount, so I was delighted when Captain and Mrs Butters offered me one of their daughter's top horses. That horse was Gunga Din, and as soon as I rode him, his way of going convinced me that his usual rider must be very talented.

His usual rider was, of course, Gonda Betrix, or Butters as she was then, a 13-year-old whose horses were prepared and presented in a highly professional manner, by herself.

As a result of her parents' offering Gunga Din to me, I came to know the Butters family quite well. We became firm friends, and I remember telling Gonda's parents that their daughter had exceptional talent and the attitude and approach that would enable her to reach the very top if she so wished.

Some months later I returned to South Africa to open the Cape Horse Show. Captain and Mrs Butters, who lived in Constantia at the time, kindly offered me horses to compete in four major classes.

It didn't worry me in the least to have to ride them over A Grade courses, because I felt confident that any horse trained by Gonda would be capable and safe. In fact, I wasn't at all surprised when the horses went so sweetly for me that they won their classes.

During my visit, Captain Butters told me he wanted to take Gonda to jump in Europe before he and his wife felt too old for the rigours of the European showjumping circuit. I considered that although Gonda was only 14, she was very mature in her approach to the sport and I told Captain Butters that I thought she could only gain from the experience. Thus assured, Gonda's parents took the plunge and her English and European season was an unqualified success.

In 1988 I returned to South Africa for a brief holiday and Gonda arranged for me to go to the Sun City Show to catch up on what was happening in the local horse world.

One of the first things I noticed was that Gonda was still producing beautifully schooled jumpers and it was a pleasure to see once again her quiet and effective style unchanged over the years. It was clear to me that her ambition and ability to win had not worn thin since we last competed together, and I wish Gonda many more seasons of success.

It has been my pleasure to write a foreword to this book, and I wish you all happy reading, patient training and good results.

As they say in Swiss: "Glück im Stall" (luck in the stable).

Pat Koechlin-Smythe

Acknowledgements

My sincere thanks to all the people who helped me to produce this book, particularly Julia Attwood-Wheeler who compiled and edited the manuscript, Dr. André Rudolph B.V. Sc. for the veterinary section, and Andrés Canovas for the farriery section.

My thanks also go to Pat Koechlin-Smythe, David and Charlotte Stubbs, to the photographer, Hennie van den Berg, and to Gary Werth for the illustrations.

Introduction

Before dealing with the training of horses, I'm going to say something about the people and horses that have influenced me and made me what I am today.

If I seem to have concentrated on the horses more than the people, it's because this book isn't meant to contain a full autobiography of my life; it outlines my training techniques. I thought, therefore, that those who may wish to read it will probably be more interested in the horses I have owned than in what my great aunt wore to a family picnic in 1903.

I think many things contribute to making us what we are: there is no doubt, for instance, that my parents did everything in their power to help me to succeed. They bought me good horses, trucked me to countless shows every year and gave me every possible encouragement to make showjumping my career.

The fact that they were a lot older than the average parents by the time I was born probably had a lot to do with the attention they paid to me. By the time they married my parents both had sons from previous marriages who were already in their twenties. When I look back, I realise that they did a lot of things with me when I was young simply because they were worried they might be too old to cope with doing them in a few years' time. I don't mean travelling to local shows of course; I mean things like taking me to England for six months after SANEF and the BHS granted me an adult licence when I was 14. Many parents would have told their child to finish school before travelling the international circuit, but I think my parents felt that even in only four years' time they might not be able to cope with living in a caravan for six months while their daughter jumped round one of the wettest countries in Europe.

But all that was in the future: better, I think, to start at the beginning.

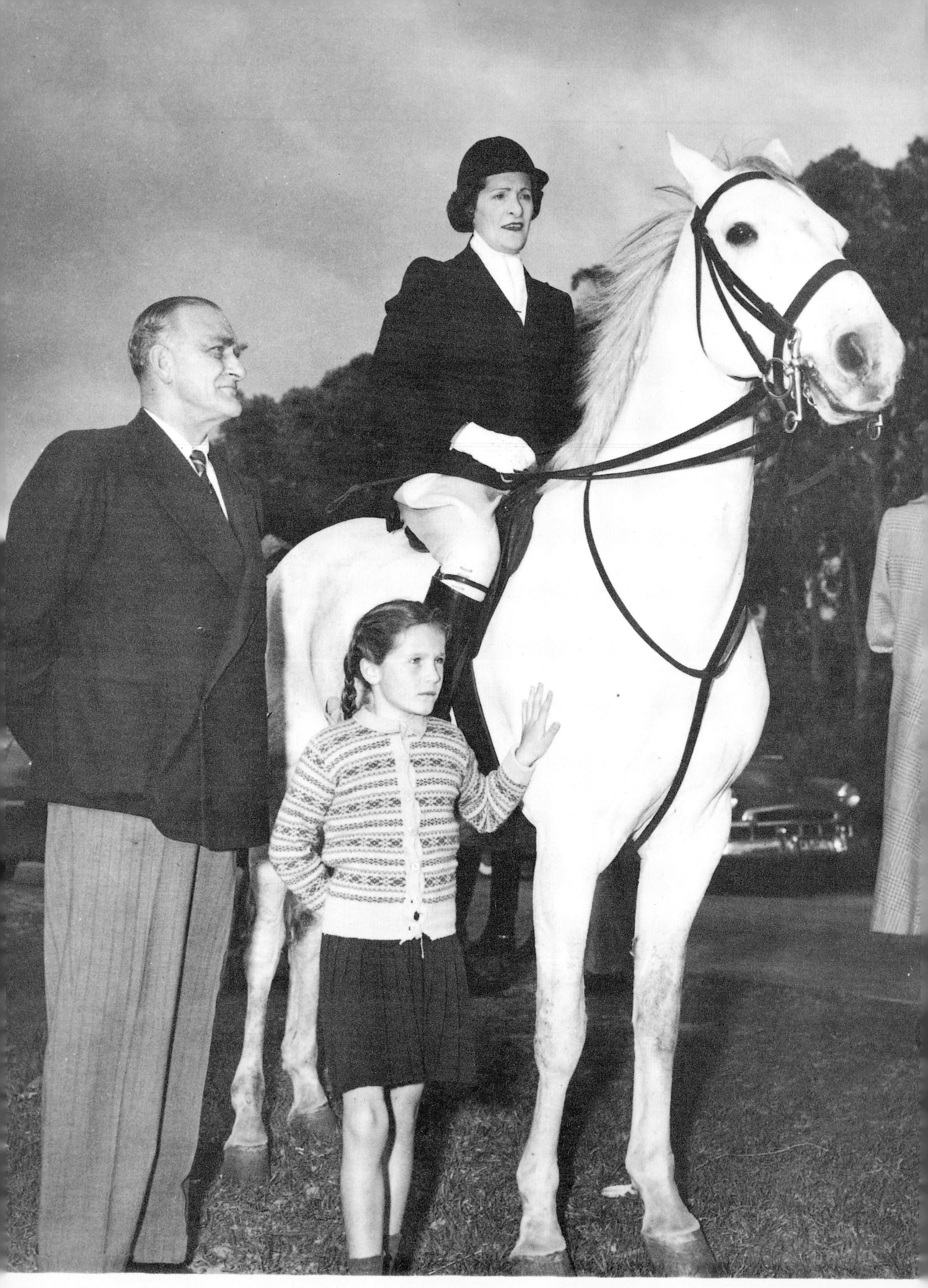

1

Early Years

A COUPLE of years after they married, my parents bought a small farm called Nahoon. It was situated in Constantia, Cape Town, and I was born there in 1943.

My father, a retired Naval Captain, ran his own import and export business and was a member of parliament so time didn't allow his interest in horses to extend beyond riding "Big Boy" as he made a weekly inspection of the farm.

My mother, on the other hand, had learned to ride as a young woman and during my childhood her interest in horses grew so that by the time I was about six, she had started buying ex-racehorses with a view to showing them.

Living on the farm made keeping the horses easy enough; the difficult bit was hiding them all from my father. Not that this deterred my mother: she simply called every horse on the place either Joie de Vivre or Coeur de Lion so that over a period of five years, my father saw a constant stream of horses which all looked pretty much the same to him; each being called either one name or the other. This way, vet bills, announcements at shows and conversations with friends raised no suspicion but my father's weekly inspection of the farm involved my mother and me in some pretty smart teamwork: no sooner had one empty outbuilding or chicken run been inspected than one or the other of us would have to move horses in there from whatever part of the farm he was about to visit next.

Needless to say, there were occasions when the family went to a horse show and sat outside the arena watching one of my mother's show horses competing in a class. After watching the horse for some minutes, my father would often pucker his brow and mutter something like, "I don't remember that horse looking quite like that . . ." And with her most disarming smile, my mother would assure him that the horse had always "looked like that" and he must be thinking of something else.

I must add that I doubt whether my father was fooled. He knew what we were up to, and I suppose he must just have decided to indulge us in the game.

Charlotte Stubbs figured prominently in my childhood. She had become a firm friend of the family when I was four years old, after my mother enlisted her help to get me back onto a pony that had given me a fright.

The pony had suddenly started to lash out or buck because, we discovered later, she had been

Left: *My parents and I*

badly torn during a difficult foaling and was often in pain.

Unfortunately we weren't aware of Beauty's problem at the time, and one afternoon she kicked out at the horse my mother was riding, causing him to throw her.

As a result, my mother broke her wrist and fractured her pelvis; she lay in the road unable to get to her feet and I had to run home for help.

I think the fact that my mother had been injured, more than anything else, gave me a fright. I remember the accident clearly but I don't remember being frightened of getting on a horse again. However, I suppose I must have been because my mother had to enlist Charlotte's help to get me back into the saddle with the promise that after ten minutes I could get off. Apparently I crouched forward with half-closed eyes and after all of ten seconds asked whether I could get off now please. However, the incident obviously didn't do me any lasting harm because I can't remember being frightened on any other occasion. In fact, I couldn't have been all that much older or bigger when I hunted on a pony called Zingela alongside my mother, right at the back of the hunt. On one occasion I saw my mother's horse slithering down an embankment and into a river, but I didn't even wait until she got out before shouting, "Are you all right?"

She spluttered, "Yes, I'm fine" so I said, "You don't mind if I go on then?" and apparently I didn't even wait for a reply before I did an about turn and took off after the hunt again. I couldn't have been more than six I suppose.

Charlotte had recently returned to South Africa after studying in Ireland with the famous Joe Hume Dudgeon. While she was in Ireland, her parents had bought a plot of land quite close to our farm and they had started to build stables on it.

Competing in my first show at 5 years of age, on Chocolate Soldier

The stables weren't complete when Charlotte came back to South Africa, so my mother offered to let her use ours for a few months.

This worked well for everyone. Charlotte had temporary stables to operate from, and my mother was now able to explain to my father that every strange horse on the farm belonged to Charlotte.

After she moved her string of horses to our stables, Charlotte gave my mother and me riding lessons. Through her I got my first really top class pony, a mare bought in Johannesburg from Derek Taylor Smith.

Derek, who is now a South African International Showjumping Judge, was then jumping in Open Adult competitions. He had jumped this mare (then called Wendy) in the Open Championships at the Rand Show. At the last jump, a single pole, the mare went underneath and Derek was left hanging over the pole, so he decided that, as he was well over 1,8 m, it might be a good idea for him to ride something slightly larger than 14h.2ins — the mare was sold to Charlotte.

Charlotte, who had me in mind when she bought the mare, renamed her Qui Va La, French for "Who Goes There". I don't know why she called her that, but I do know that every horse or pony in Charlotte's stable had to have a name ending in *a*.

It seemed to my mother that there was little Qui Va La couldn't do. As well as showjumping, she had proved herself across country and in the showing arena. Also, she was the first pony we'd come across who could do flying changes in a straight line. We were *terribly* impressed with that!

My mother paid £100 for her, a

lot of money in those days. Some top showjumpers went for less, and perhaps I felt slightly overawed by her, I don't know, but I was reluctant to ride Qui Va La at first. I think it was because she was so good, and also much stronger than any of my previous ponies.

My mother didn't push me to get on this pony for which she'd just paid a fortune, although one could have forgiven her for having a fit under the circumstances. Instead, she just left me alone until, one evening, I came home from school and slipped a halter onto Qui Va La. Then I led her up to a fence and scrambled onto her much to the delight of my mother who found me trotting her bareback round the paddock a short while later.

One might expect that some major win would have been the thing to spark off my desire to make a career of showjumping, but that isn't so. For some reason, it was having the courage to get on Qui Va La that marked a real turning point for me.

Qui Va La at the Rosebank Show in 1951

At about this time, my mother's show horses were doing particularly well. In the 1960s she swept the board for three years running, winning every Show Championship in the country on a first-class dressage horse called Quick Silver.

My mother was also showjumping in those days, and although she was almost 50, she thought nothing of jumping a course of 1,37 m. I think that was a considerable achievement for a woman who didn't start competing until she was in her mid-40s, and I doubt whether I'd have been able to accomplish that if I'd started jumping at the age I am now.

My father had his 66th birthday in 1956 and shortly afterwards, he sold the major portion of our 12 ha farm.

With it went the main house, so my father took us to England for three months while a cottage was being renovated and stables were built on the remaining few acres.

When Charlotte discovered that I would be in England for three months, she advised my mother to book me in for a month's tuition with the late Col Dudgeon, and I was fortunate enough to have two lessons and two lectures a day from this great old horseman.

It was hard going. I was only 12, and after the lessons I stayed on to muck out, clean tack and groom horses.

My mother had booked us into an inn close by, and every day we caught a bus that dropped us off somewhere near the stables. She had decided to improve her dressage while I was learning more about my trade, and one of the things I remember particularly well is watching Penny Morton (a top dressage rider at the time) give a demonstration on one of her horses.

During the demonstration she executed a dressage test, jumped a course of 1,2 m jumps, popped over a row of artificial swords and finished by jumping onto a portable bank (which was about 1,1 m^2) before halting her horse. This would have been impressive enough under ordinary circumstances, but Penny Morton did it all bareback and without a bridle.

Not to be outdone, Charlotte Stubbs taught her own horse a similar routine, which she performed at shows in and around the Cape as a demonstration of horse control.

Col Dudgeon's instruction was tough, but at the end of the month he told my parents that he felt I had ability. He went on to say that if they didn't push me, I'd be of an international standard by the time I was 14.

When my parents asked him why they mustn't push me, he said that many children are spoiled by their parents who turn the sport into a nightmare for them. I think the same is true today; probably more so because the prize money is bigger and so is the pressure for the child to win, especially if a parent has paid a fortune for a junior A Grade.

The first show I went to after our return from England was at the Cape Hunt and Polo Field. It was there that my mother saw a horse being jumped in the C Grade by the late David Burgess, a local vet. He and his wife Pat had purchased the horse, a part-bred Hackney, from a farm in Worcester where he had become a great nuisance to his owner by jumping out of every paddock on the farm.

David had called the horse Gunga Din, and my mother took an instant liking to him. She also felt that as I had shot up in height (I was now 1,7 m and weighed 63,5 kg), Qui Va La would soon be outgrown.

David had bought the horse for his wife who was one of the leading showjumpers in the Cape at that time, and he didn't want to sell, so my mother asked for an option in the event of his changing his mind.

Unfortunately, it seemed that even an option was out of the question. Yvonne Garratt, daughter of the late Sid Garratt (who was one of this country's most famous racehorse trainers), had already secured first option.

Eventually, David decided to sell Gunga Din and Yvonne Garratt was heartbroken when her father refused to buy him: like many racehorse trainers, he couldn't see any point in buying something he couldn't race and her loss was our gain when David offered the horse to us.

In a gesture really quite out of character, my father bought Gunga Din himself and gave him to me. I think that was a turning point for him because from then on, he took full interest in my riding career. Perhaps he thought, "If you can't beat 'em, join 'em." I don't know.

These days, when a child's parents have paid a large sum of money for a top junior horse, people expect the child to do well, but secretly hope he or she will do badly, I think. In much the same way, a few eyebrows were raised when it was learned that my parents had paid £200 for Gunga Din. It simply wasn't done in those days, and I became keenly aware of being watched.

I had long since moved into Junior classes, and in those days, Juniors could ride in Open Adult competitions. However, I wasn't allowed to compete in certain adult competitions and if there was a class my mother and I thought Gunga Din could compete in, he was ridden by either Yvonne Garratt or Pat Burgess.

While it is true that riding Qui Va La had been the turning point in my wanting to make show-jumping my career, I think it was Gunga Din who taught me that if I was to succeed, I must be dedicated. He wasn't an easy horse, very strong and difficult to hold. He wasn't too bad in the ring, but at home he often took off with me and would tear round and round the paddock while I attempted to bring him under some sort of control.

It was gratifying when the hard work paid off: at the Port Elizabeth Agricultural Show in 1957, Gunga Din and Qui Va La cleaned up for me. Qui excelled in the dressage and showing classes, and Gunga Din took a place in nearly all the open classes when he competed successfully against the late Bob Grayston, David Stubbs, Willie Angus and Georgie Peerman.

I was lucky of course, but I had also put a tremendous amount of work into those horses, having finally learned that they wouldn't do it on their own.

It was just as well that this message had finally sunk in because in April 1957 my mother and I saw a 14h.3½ins chestnut gelding as we drove into the showgrounds at the Bloemfontein Agricultural Show. He was being jumped in the practice arena by Ben van Vuuren, and he had such a striking jump that we sat and watched.

Helen Swann, a local and highly knowledgeable horsewoman, noticed our interest and began to tell us what she knew of the horse.

We learned that he had walked 20 km to the show without shoes, and that when he wasn't competing, he had to stand in bran poultices because his feet were so badly worn down. Apparently, his owner lived in the middle of the bush and could rarely get hold of a farrier.

Despite this, he competed in the adult competitions and was in the Orange Free State Interprovincial Team Championship which was held on the last day of the show.

This horse was, of course, Oorskiet, a totally unschooled character who had the disconcerting habit of putting his head in the air and flybucking out of the ring when he went past the exit. He was frequently eliminated as a result, but in spite of all that my mother and I were mad about him.

If Helen Swann thought we were crazy, she disguised the fact politely and secured an option on him for us.

My father, meanwhile, said absolutely nothing about the horse. He had seen some of Oorskiet's antics and when he learned about the option, he made it abundantly clear that the horse would be bought over his dead body.

That seemed to be the end of the matter since once my father had made up his mind, there was no budging him and there was therefore no point in making a fuss about it.

I wasn't allowed to ride in the Interprovincial Team Championship and my father, mother and I were sitting on the stand. Bob Grayston, riding Captain Bligh, and Pat Burgess, riding Gunga Din, proved to be the only two to go clear. The bogey appeared to be a treble combination and when Oorskiet entered the arena, I turned to my father and said, "If Oorskiet jumps that combination . . . can I have him?"

My father considered for what seemed a lifetime. He knew that Oorskiet was only a C Grade, and I discovered later that he was trying to decide whether he was likely to clear the treble. After deciding that there wasn't even the faintest chance that a mad unschooled horse would succeed where sensible and experienced horses had failed, he replied, "Of course."

I immediately said, "Do you promise?" And such was my father's confidence, he said, "Yes. I promise," which is why, when Oorskiet sailed over the treble with feet to spare, the colour drained from his face. Being a man of his word, he was then forced to agree to buying Oorskiet for me and we rushed down to have him measured, just to be sure he *was* only 14h3ins. If he had been taller, I wouldn't have been able to ride him in juniors, but as it turned out, I never rode him in juniors anyway: I competed with him in open adult.

When the purchase was agreed subject to vet, I couldn't believe my luck, but was so positive Oorskiet would fail the vet or something equally disappointing, I hardly dared breathe until we'd loaded him into the train which was to take him and Gunga Din back to the Western Province.

My mother and I met the train at the other end. We'd taken a blanket to throw over him, scared to death in case anyone who saw us walking this scarecrow back to our stable thought we were responsible for the state he was in.

Oorskiet, thin and still very much unschooled, at a small show several weeks after we bought him

It was only later I discovered that Oorskiet means "left overs" in Afrikaans. In view of his overall condition, I had to admit that the name fitted him rather well; particularly when it came to light that he had once been swapped for a cow at a farm in the Free State and that he had then ended up at a livestock auction where nobody bid for him.

Ben van Vuuren had felt sorry for little Oorskiet who looked like a horse but measured as a pony, and he bought him for £12.

He really was "left overs".

2

Oorskiet and Gunga Din

WHEN I grew too tall for Qui Va La, my mother and I wondered what to do with her. We didn't really want to sell her because she had done everything for me, and despite having Gunga Din and Oorskiet, I couldn't bear the thought of letting her go.

In the end, my mother loaned her to Janie Myburg who was then a junior, and Janie made her debut on Qui before we sold her to the Wright family in 1959.

At that time, Gillian and Judy Wright weren't really pupils of mine — I was after all only 16 — but my mother and I helped the two girls who sailed through the junior grades before retiring Qui to a farm in the Eastern Cape a good few years later.

I spent a great deal of time schooling Oorskiet, who knew absolutely nothing. His mouth was as dead as a doornail on one side and he was totally undisciplined. His mouth I could do little about because it had been spoiled, and I was never able to ride him in a snaffle; but firmness and a total determination not to let him do as he liked did at least result in his learning a few manners — though not many. He still often flybucked his way to the exit when in the ring, and he might have defeated me totally if it had not been for Bob Grayston and my mother standing at the exit one day and belting him across the bottom with branches taken from a thorn bush. These were indeed desperate measures, but Oorskiet's behaviour warranted them, and after a few episodes, he simply gave up and never did it again.

Oorskiet at the Goodwood Show, seven months after we bought him

I was pleased about that because a short while later Pat Smythe visited South Africa and the thought of her witnessing me being flybucked out of the arena was just too embarrassing to contemplate.

Pat was already famous in the world of showjumping, her horses Tosca and Prince Hal being household names. I spent her entire visit mortified with shyness because she was staying at our home while in the Cape, and I was both pleased and terrified when my father loaned her Gunga Din so that she could compete in the adult classes at the Pretoria Agricultural Show.

I was not allowed to ride in some of the adult classes, but rode Oorskiet and one of my mother's horses, Drambuie, to compete against her in the open and unrestricted adult classes.

I was fortunate enough to win a gold medal for Rider of the Show that year, and Pat advised my parents to apply to the South

African National Equestrian Federation (SANEF) for an adult licence.

SANEF granted the licence and asked the British Horse Society to do the same so that I could also compete as an adult in England. Fortunately for me, the British Horse Society agreed to SANEF's request and in 1958 the licence was granted.

At that time, I was just some little pipsqueak who had mustered sufficient cheek to compete in an Adult High Jump at the Rand Show. The high jump record, which was held by Bob Grayston, stood at 6′8″ (2,03 m); somehow Gunga Din managed to break the record by clearing 6′10″ (2,08 m). Our success was short lived, however, because I faulted at 7′ (2,13 m), which Bob immediately cleared to regain his title.

Gunga Din clears 6′10″ (2,08 m) in the Adult High Jump at the Rand Show in 1958

Incidentally, Oorskiet, who as you know was a mere 14h.3, also competed in the high jump and cleared 6′8″ (2,03 m) before faulting at 6′10″ (2,08 m). A remarkable feat for such a little guy.

Not to be deterred, Oorskiet and I went on to win the Rand Show Championship the following day, and Gunga Din was runner-up — something no other rider had achieved before, and a trick I was to repeat in 1979 with Country Cottage and Honey Girl.

Shortly afterwards, my mother, father, Oorskiet and Gunga Din set sail for England with a very nervous 14-year-old who was to fulfil Col Dudgeon's expectation: *that she would become an international rider within two years if not pushed.*

3

ENGLAND

IT'S 33 years since I went to England as a 14-year-old and naturally, the show-jumping circuit was rather different in those days.

To give you an idea of the sort of era I'm talking of, I've listed a few of the people who were jumping the circuit at that time. Many of them will still be known to you today. In fact, some of them are still going, and are even greater characters than they were then: Pat Smythe, Ted Edgar, Peter Robeson, Alan Oliver, Ted Williams, David Broome, George Hobbs and, of course, the inimitable Harvey Smith. (This was slightly before Anneli's time, so don't think I've forgotten her, but she wasn't showjumping when I was 14 — she was eventing.)

Travelling the horses to England had been an absolute nightmare. We sailed, of course, and it was quite a performance to get me, my parents, the car, three horses and all the accompanying equipment onto the ship.

In order to get the horses aboard, they first had to be loaded individually into a crate. The crate was to be lifted and swung over the hull of the ship before being gently delivered on deck and because my mother didn't like the idea of the horses being alone during this ordeal, she asked one of our African grooms to climb into the crate with the first horse. The crate was then lifted over the hull and when it was opened up some minutes later, we found the groom frozen to the spot with terror. It took a lot of coaxing from us before he would venture out onto the deck and I don't think he ever got over it.

Horses could only travel on ships with a "well" deck which allowed the boxes to be secured and given protection from the weather; the *Arundel Castle* was such a ship.

We had enlisted a top-class English groom to help us during our journey and subsequent tour of the showjumping circuit; her name was Rosemary Head, and she was one of the most capable people I've ever come across. There seemed to be nothing she didn't know about travelling and grooming horses, but this should have come as no surprise because she'd groomed for Phil Oliver (Alan Oliver's father), Harry Llewellyn and Bob Grayston among others.

If not for Rosemary, we might never have thought of taking the sort of medical supplies she forced us to pack; much less the very basic but equally important Epsom salts and bicarbonate of soda which she fed to the horses every couple of days to keep their digestive systems in order. It was to be a tedious 14 days, and we had to be sure that we had sufficient supplies to see us through the journey. Trying to think of every conceivable item we might need was nerve-wracking.

Rosemary was given special permission to go into the well deck with the horses because the shipping regulations forbade passengers in this area. I was also allowed down and often found her there, grooming and massaging the horses to keep them fit. I tried to give a hand myself but I couldn't do it as well as she could with all her years of experience.

I can't tell you the relief when we finally docked at Southampton: I was fed up with the ship, the sea, the food — and talking of food, we had to throw all the unused fodder overboard before we docked.

Rosemary had organised the purchase of a three-berth horsebox which had been kindly provided by Harry Llewellyn. It wasn't quite fitted out as a horsebox, but with some alterations it was fine. I think we paid £400 for it, which was quite a lot of money, but fortunately we sold it for the same at the end of our tour.

My father had arranged accommodation in a small inn quite close to the first show I was to compete in, which happened to be the Royal Windsor Horse Show.

Thanks to Rosemary's careful feeding and massage, the horses were still fit enough to jump and seven days after arriving in England, I found myself trailing around the showground in a state of extreme nervousness.

I recognised many of the international riders but I was far too shy to say a word to them because I really felt like a little pipsqueak. I couldn't even bring myself to say hello to Pat Smythe, despite the fact that she had stayed with my family only months before, and when I realised I'd in effect cut her dead I was upset in case she thought this was my intention.

Gunga Din competing in England

In the end, I hung around the collecting ring waiting for the bell to indicate that the competitors could walk the course. The jumps looked pretty huge and I was just contemplating this fact when Alan Oliver tapped me on the shoulder. "Are you the little girl from South Africa?"

I nodded dumbly.

"Would you like to walk the course with me?" he said, and he smiled at me kindly.

"Yes please," I whispered, so totally overawed I could hardly get the words out.

He took me through every stride, offering as much help as he possibly could, and I have never forgotten his kindness. He was one of the world's greatest riders, but he took the trouble to help me at a time when he could have been forgiven for devoting his entire attention to what lay ahead of him in the competition.

I was to jump both Gunga Din and Oorskiet in that class, and Gunga Din soon became one of only eight clear rounds out of 50 entries. The course was pretty tough! I wondered how Oorskiet would handle it, and was just about to enter the ring on him when a marshall pulled me up and said "When you rode Gunga Din earlier, you forgot to salute the Queen!"

I just wanted the ground to open up and swallow me. I don't know how I got round the course and was hardly even aware that I'd had 16 faults, so great was my embarrassment. Later, I asked my father if the Queen would be cross with me and he replied, "No, I'm sure she'll forgive you; she knows it was a mistake."

I had pulled myself together by the time the jump-off came, and when Gunga Din had only four faults, the media commented favourably on our performance.

The next major show was in Plymouth. Rosemary drove the horsebox and by this time we had acquired a caravan which we pitched in the showgrounds. We had forgotten, of course, that this was England and not South Africa; that it rained almost every day. Towing the caravan into and out of muddy showgrounds was to become an experience none of us would ever forget.

In Plymouth, the rain poured relentlessly down and the caravan started to sink. I hadn't quite mastered walking in wellingtons with several kilograms of mud clinging to each heel, and my parents and I had begun to feel distinctly cold and miserable. I cheered up a bit when I discovered that I'd been put on a poster advertising the show. In fact, I was so chuffed I kept stealing all the posters; it's a wonder anybody ever knew the show was on!

The horses were stabled in temporary constructions which were protected from the elements by large tents. We were to discover that most of the shows accommodated the horses in this way, and they seemed happy enough. We, on the other hand, were struggling a bit in our caravan. Although we were one of an entourage that had been accommodated in a field close to the stables, the day to day problem of how to dry wet clothes in front of a tiny gas stove made me appreciate how well off I had been at home! The facilities, wherever we camped, were limited to say the least.

We later calculated that we had covered about 10 000 km during our stay in England and my wins and placings gave me a total of £1 500 in prize money. In those days, the winner of any big event received only £100 (although this was worth a lot then of course) and my winnings went quite some way towards helping to offset the cost of the trip.

Certain things stand out in my mind, such as the incident following my win at Brighton at the South of England Championship when I beat Pat Smythe into second place; after the event, a journalist asked me how many times I had beaten Pat and I replied that she had beaten me many more times than I had beaten her. In later years, as I searched through the notes my father had written during our stay in England, I was touched to read that he had written of that occasion, "It is nice to see that Gonda hasn't got a swollen head!"

There were funny incidents too: at one of the shows, my father was standing behind two women who were watching me jump. Said one to the other, "They say she's only 14." Then she nodded towards me and continued, "She'll never see 20 again!"

I also learned a harsh lesson within months of travelling the circuit. While competing in a class that offered prize money of £100, I was one of three riders to go into the jump-off and shortly before the class, one of the other two riders approached me and said, "Listen. Our horses are tired and I'm sure Oorskiet is too."

"What of it?" I wanted to know.

He paused for thought and then smiled. "I don't know if you know," he said, "but in England, it's common practice for the riders to arrange to fluff the class so that none of them wins, otherwise we could go on and on competing in jump-off after jump-off. What's the point?"

I didn't answer, so he went on, "How about if we all make a mess of our jump-off, and then we split the money?"

I wasn't sure what to make of this. I hadn't been in England long, and the man talking to me was a top class international rider. I didn't want to do anything that would make me unpopular. If this sort of thing really *was* frequently done in England, perhaps I ought to play along to keep the peace?

Before I could say anything, he suggested that I should fail to go through the start, which would cause me to be eliminated, and he assured me that his friend would take the wrong course while *he* would retire.

I didn't like the sound of it, but he assured me it would be all right, so like a fool I agreed.

You can probably guess what happened next: following my elimination, he and his friend fought hell for leather for that £100. To give them their due, they did give me my share of it, the whole point of the exercise being that the class was a qualifier for something else. What they'd really been trying to do was to get me out of the way so that they could grab a few extra points

THE CAPE ARGUS, WEDNESDAY, JUNE 18, 1958

'Let's face it, chaps; this girl on Gunga Din is a better man than we are!'

while I was put down a place or so.

My father was furious, and despite my attempts at an explanation he hit the roof. "It serves you right," he told me. "I hope this will teach you that honesty is the best policy — don't ever try to cheat again."

I was horrified. I hadn't thought of myself as cheating anybody of anything, and then I realised he was right. It was a hard lesson, but one worth learning.

On the lighter side, I must say that during that trip, Paddy McMahon became my hero. He was very good to me and when I struck a problem with Gunga Din (who had started standing off too far), it was Paddy who came to the rescue and helped me overcome it. I idolised him in the way a 14-year-old might idolise a pop star today and the absolute high spot of my entire English trip was not that I came second to Paddy in the British National Championships, but that Paddy asked me to share with him the front carriage of the Blackpool Grand National Roller Coaster that evening when a crowd of us went to the fair. The thought of actually sitting next to him was too wonderful for words, and he patted my arm in a fatherly manner as he tucked me into the carriage that would give me the best ride!

Now, when I look back, I realise that of all the people competing at top level in those days, there's only David Broom and Harvey Smith left. There's me, of course, but I'm not in England. Had I been in England all my life, however, I'm certain that I would at least have tried to stay at the top just the same. I think I would have succeeded too, because whereas many top riders eventually get tired of the circuit and give it up to do something else, that's never happened to me. I never get tired of competing, and I've never lost my desire to win. However, winning is a byproduct of an even greater desire; something I hope I will never get bored with as long as I live — that of getting a horse going properly, of getting it to perform to its greatest ability; to fulfil its potential; to *succeed.*

4

Parting with Oorskiet

IT WAS April 1958 when I went to England. As I mentioned before, I had been granted a licence to compete there as an adult. However, I had to compete in Europe as a junior and after leaving England to compete in Hanover and Rotterdam, I joined the South African junior team of Tony Lewis and George Myburg, Yvonne Peterson and the late Rory Donnellan, who was captain.

In Hanover we tied with the Italian team for second place after being narrowly beaten by the British who won with a score of three faults to our four. But in Rotterdam our team won, and much to our delight, both George and I also managed to win individual competitions.

The rest of the junior team then returned to South Africa, but because of the licence allowing me to jump as an adult in England, I returned to Britain to compete there again.

The Showjumper of the Year Show at Haringey was to be my last show before I too went home and it was here that the Duchess of Norfolk approached my mother and asked whether we would sell Oorskiet.

The Duchess of Norfolk had first seen Oorskiet in Germany after I had lent him to George Myburg who was in the junior team. To see George now, at 1,9 m, it's hard to believe, but he was quite short in those days, and after his impressive win on Oorskiet, the Duchess decided that she must have Oorskiet for her daughter.

Lady Sarah Fitzallan-Howard was a keen rider (which was probably just as well in view of her mother's decision that she should have Oorskiet), and she was a member of the junior British Team. Consequently, the Duchess was always on the lookout for good horses for her and she repeatedly approached my mother in the hope of wearing her down. However, my mother would have none of it. "Oorskiet isn't for sale," she kept saying.

The Duchess simply wouldn't take no for an answer. She kept on and on asking and my mother kept on and on refusing so that I half wondered whether we'd get on the ship to sail for home and find the Duchess of Norfolk under the bed in the cabin.

On the second last day of Haringey, I was invited to compete in the International Knock-Out Pairs. The top 16 or 20 riders of the show were invited to compete in this event and I was given a special dispensation to enable me to compete, because my adult licence allowed me to compete only in the national events and not in the international ones. Fortunately for me, after many rounds, Oorskiet came out victorious: I beat Carlos Figaro of Spain into second place. And who should be waiting for my mother as I came out of the ring but the Duchess of Norfolk, once again saying, "I have to have that horse for my daughter. I have to!"

My mother was getting very tired of this, so she turned to her and said, "All right then. But you're mad if you even consider paying what we're going to ask because we won't take a penny less than £5 000." (I must add that, later on, my mother was rather embarrassed at having spoken to the Duchess like that. It was just that she'd asked so often, my mother eventually snapped.)

£5 000 was a lot of money in those days — it's no small amount now — and as a matter of interest, our entire six-month trip with all the expense of travelling ourselves and the horses had cost £7 500.

Actually, the night before we had held a family conference in the caravan, and we had decided that in view of what the trip had cost, perhaps we would be wise to let Oorskiet go if the Duchess was prepared to pay £5 000. Then we all laughed because we thought that nobody would dream of paying such a sum, so we were dumbstruck when the Duchess of Norfolk said, "Done!"

My mother went quite pale. "You're mad if you're willing to pay five thousand," she repeated, but the Duchess opened her handbag to take out her chequebook. My mother suddenly tried to make her clasp the bag shut. "No!" she said. "We can't sell him just like that. We need another 24 hours to think about it." But after much discussion, we decided we couldn't turn the offer down, and although it was a sad moment when the deal was done, we at least knew that little "left overs" would have a wonderful home for life.

He went on to win many more championships with Lady Sarah who won the Leading Lady Rider in Great Britain and on the continent and represented Great Britain on many occasions with Oorskiet. We, however, learned a hard lesson after selling him, for it took a year or more to find a replacement. Our problem was made worse by the fact that during the voyage home, the ship was hit by a large wave and as a result, Gunga Din fell in his box injuring his shoulder. We only discovered that he'd hurt himself several weeks after we arrived back in Cape Town when we tried to work him only to discover that he was lame. Gunga Din was out of action for three or four months, and because I'd sold Oorskiet, I didn't have a top horse to compete on.

It was partly for this reason that we bought Flyridge from Joyce and Terence Millard. Terence Millard is today a highly successful racehorse trainer, but many years ago he was a showjumper. I clearly remember watching him compete at the Rosebank Show and at the Cape Hunt Polo Club when I was quite small.

His wife, Joyce, had trained and jumped Flyridge, who was an A Grade when we first saw him. Once again I must stress that I was very lucky to have parents who were 100% behind me; I think they knew that if I had a gap in my career at that stage, I was at an age when I might lose interest in showjumping, so they bought Flyridge and I had five or six very successful years with him.

5

Eldorado and Ratification

AFTER Flyridge came two wonderful horses: Eldorado and Ratification. Ratification had been bought through Edgar Potts, a man I'd met through my interest in amateur racing.

When I was 12, I'd started riding work for Gail Thompson and at 17, I was offered a ride in the Cape Hunt Race on a horse Edgar was training, so arrangements were made for me to meet him and ride work for him.

Eldorado, winner of the 1967 Derby

He wasn't terribly reliable: the first day I was to ride for him, he left me hanging around Kenilworth racecourse for an hour and I decided to go home, but as I drove out of the racecourse, I saw a man walking down the road towards me. I wound down the window and asked him if he was Edgar Potts. He was, and I then proceeded to tell him what I thought of him being late. Even so, he managed to persuade me to go back to the racecourse with him where I rode several of his horses.

I've often wondered what might have happened if I'd refused to go back, because by the time two months had passed, I was thoroughly involved with him.

My parents were horrified, and to be fair, although I thought they were being unreasonable at the time, I have to admit that over the years I've come to understand why: Edgar was 12 years older than I; he found it difficult to hold down a steady job; he drank more than was good for him, and he encouraged me to do things I shouldn't have been doing at 17. That said, even my parents had to admit that he was an absolute genius with horses. Today, I can glance over a stable door as I walk past and in those few seconds notice a splint develop-

Winning the Ladies Flat Race at the Cape Hunt and Polo Club Amateur Race Meeting at Kenilworth

ing, a slight swelling on any part of the leg or a knock that wasn't there even five minutes earlier, and it was Edgar who taught me to be so observant. He used to notice things about horses that even a vet couldn't pick up without a thorough examination, and he had a wonderful knack of treating leg problems with old-fashioned remedies.

People like that are very gifted and also very few and far between. The pity of it with Edgar is that he didn't try to put his gift to better use half the time, but that didn't put me off him when I was 17.

Within weeks I'd forgotten all about showjumping. My horses were standing in the paddock, not having even seen a jump since I met Edgar, while I was spending all my time either at the racetrack or at Edgar's stables.

After two months of this my parents had had enough and they put their foot down. Either you stop seeing him, they said, or we'll sell your horses.

At the time, I had Eldorado, Ratification and Flyridge, so I was fairly confident that even in their irate state, my parents wouldn't be angry enough to sell those; but I was wrong.

My parents' threats went on for at least a year, during which time I did in fact ride and compete the horses, but I was still spending all my spare time with Edgar and my parents didn't approve. Needless to say, I wouldn't change; eventually I left home after a particularly bad row about Edgar. I went to live in a rented flat close to the racecourse.

One night, my parents hammered on the door and when I opened it, they told me that they had arranged for Eldorado, Ratification and Flyridge to be sold to Jackie Bader, a South African rider who had emigrated to Italy.

To say that I had a fit would be putting it mildly. My parents had come, not to inform me politely so much as to *tell* me to put my signature to the deed of sale. In the back of my mind, I always knew that I wanted to make showjumping my career, and when my parents made it clear that I must sort myself out or the horses would have to go, I went home.

It was at about that time that my father had a man-to-man talk with Edgar Potts. He explained that as Edgar was 12 years older than I, perhaps it would be a good idea to give me a bit of a breathing space; a chance to grow up a bit more and decide what I really wanted to do with my life.

Edgar naturally wanted to know what he was supposed to do in the meantime and my father suggested he should go into the army. He said that rather than joining for one year's national service, Edgar should join the permanent force for two years and that if he proved that he could settle down and make something of himself, my father would reconsider how he felt about our relationship.

My father had many connections in the government and after Edgar eventually agreed to the plan, it wasn't difficult to get the paperwork adjusted so that Edgar unwittingly committed himself for five years instead of two.

When Edgar found out what had happened, he thought at first that it was a mistake and he asked his commanding officer to do something to put it right. However, his commanding officer merely pointed out that there was something else Edgar ought to know: he'd been posted to Grahamstown for the entire five years!

After the initial shock wore off, Edgar decided to look at the whole thing logically. He knew there had to be some way of getting himself out of Grahamstown, and there was: some months later, he married an old flame of his, and as per the rules, the army posted him back to the Cape so that he could be closer to his wife.

Even so, we remained friends, and as I mentioned earlier, it was through Edgar that I had found Ratification after he'd phoned me one day to say that he had a horse that kept jumping a tricky fence so that he could get into a neighbouring field.

I thought that even if the horse wouldn't do for me, he might do for a pupil of mine who was looking for a horse at the time, but when I first set eyes on Ratification, I thought he looked like a bit of a pony. He had a bushy mane and tail and was very compact which made him look small.

Edgar persuaded the owner to let me have him at home for a week's trial and after two days of work he was jumping over fences of 0,91 m to 1 m, so I phoned my pupil and suggested that she come to see him.

My pupil came but actually showed little interest as she had some friends with her and seemed to prefer chatting to them to looking at Ratification.

Ratification felt good to me, and although he was only three days under saddle as a jumper, I decided to raise the jumps to 1,07 m and 1,14 m respectively — just to see how he would react to them.

When he soared over the jumps at their new height, I suddenly realised what a good little horse I was sitting on, so I got the measuring stick out and after discovering that he was 16 hands, I decided to buy him for myself (for the vast sum of R100) especially as my pupil didn't seem to be showing much interest.

With training and work, Ratification went on to become highly successful. He won the South African Championship twice, was runner-up in the Derby, was a silver medallist at the SA Games and won many a Grand Prix and Championship. In fact, he and Eldorado used to fight out a lot of competitions and I remember one year at the Rand Easter Show when Eldorado and Ratification won the first six out of eight competitions.

Eldorado had also been an amateur racehorse before he came to me. He was originally named Moonlight and I first saw him bush-racing at gymkhanas around the Cape. I wanted him straight away, but Janie Myburg had seen him before me and she had secured an option on him.

At the Rawsonville gymkhana, Moonlight won the Ladies Race, the Junior Race, the Five Furlong, the

Mile and the Three Furlong Scurry all in the same day — quite an achievement to say the least!

It was at the end of this gymkhana that Janie managed to persuade the owners to sell him to her for R35, but the sale went through on one condition: Moonlight's name had to be changed.

Both Janie and I have often thought this an odd condition of sale. The only possible explanation would be that the owners didn't want the horse recognised or his true identity revealed. Stranger still was the fact that when I later tried to look up Moonlight's pedigree and track record, it was as though he'd never existed, and I never did find out his true identity.

Janie changed his name to Eldorado and kept him for about six months, during which time she started to train him as a showjumper. However, Janie was very small and light and Eldorado continually tried to take advantage of her. Sometimes he would just grind to a halt and put his head in the air defying Janie to do anything about it, and if she gave him a belt with her crop, he'd then try to buck her off.

At about that time, Janie's parents suggested that she should go to Germany to study for a year. Because she thought it would be unwise for her to have Eldorado just hanging around doing nothing, Janie offered to sell him to me and I bought him for R50.

Eldorado went on to win many major competitions for me during the 1960s. He won the SA Championship in 1965 (at his first A Grade show) and gave me my first Derby win in 1967. He also won the Grand Prix at the Rand Show several times, was a gold medallist at the SA Games and won the Showjumper of the Year. In all, he was undoubtedly one of the best horses in the country at the time. But just before the 1967 Rand Show, Eldorado slipped with me into a jump and fell with his hindquarters landing on my leg, breaking my left ankle. At the same time he injured one of his tendons and put himself out of work for six months.

It was only eight weeks to the Rand Show and I wasn't terribly impressed by this. With a fractured ankle encased in a plaster cast, I had little chance of competing that year. Nevertheless, I sent Ratification and Flyridge up to the Rand Show just in case some miracle mended my leg and enabled me to ride.

I was still living in the Cape at the time and, whenever I was competing my horses in the Transvaal, I travelled them by train. This entailed riding the horses from Johannesburg station to wherever the show was, which was often as far afield as Inanda. The traffic wasn't so hectic in those days of course, but even so, it was a considerable distance to have to hack and needless to say, the horses had to arrive some days before the show was due to start to give them a chance to recover from the journey prior to competing.

I didn't travel by train myself: my parents drove me around until I was old enough to drive myself and then I usually drove through the night in time to meet my horses at the station. In fact, I've travelled the Cape to Johannesburg road so many times I could be forgiven for never wanting to see it again. As a result, one of my pet hates is driving long distances.

The world-famous German showjumper, Hans Günter Winkler, had been invited to compete in South Africa at the time that my leg was in plaster, and as the authorities were looking for good horses for him to ride, I naturally offered Ratification. I held Flyridge back in the hope that if only I could get rid of the plaster cast, I might at least be able to ride on the last two days of the show.

To cut a long story short, Ratification seemed to take an instant dislike to Hans Winkler. This was both embarrassing and quite incredible, because there is no doubt that Hans Winkler is still today recognised as having been one of the greatest riders the world has ever seen.

I tried to explain this to Rats but he wouldn't listen. He continued to be as awkward as possible with Hans, even stopping with him at fences of less than 1,2 m.

I remember going up to Hans and suggesting that he give Rats a good hiding, which he did, but it didn't help. Ratification had made up his mind that he wasn't going to jump for Hans, and that was that! I hated to think what such a famous rider thought of this so-called top showjumper and I could see by his face that he wasn't impressed. Nor was he impressed with my offering Rats for him to ride!

All this happened two days before the Rand Show was due to start and that evening I borrowed a pair of scissors from a great friend of mine, Lynda Kirschman. I then soaked my leg in a bath of hot water and between the two of us, we hacked the plaster off my leg. Unfortunately what came out of the plaster wasn't a foot at all! It was a funny little leg with a floppy foot hanging on the end of it.

However, I was now determined to ride the rejected Ratification at the show come what may, and I spent the whole of the next day on crutches, putting my foot on the ground, putting weight slowly on it, and beginning to walk on it. Then I went for an X-ray.

Fortunately the X-ray showed that the bone had healed, so with great reluctance my doctor told me I could ride providing I strapped my ankle up solidly with an elastic bandage. He thought I was crazy even to consider riding (I hadn't mentioned jumping!), but not being a rider himself, he couldn't grasp what it meant to me.

My parents were in Cape Town at the time and knew nothing of what was going on. I certainly wasn't going to tell them and later that day, I bought myself a pair of long black socks and a veldskoen shoe which I covered in black boot polish.

I needed permission from the judges before I could ride in a competition with my left leg out of a riding boot, and I suppose they weren't too impressed by the prospect of me competing with my leg in a long sock and a veldskoen, but they agreed to let me try.

My leg was pretty useless to tell the truth, and I couldn't take much weight on it at all. I wasn't even walking on it properly but, all the same, I got on Ratification before the first competition, warmed him up, and in I went.

If I remember correctly, we took a fairly low ticket in the first two competitions, but on the last three

Ratification clears the water jump at the Rand Show

days Ratification and I went on to win the Grand Prix, the Henessy Championship and the South African National Championship, much to the surprise of Hans Günter Winkler who said, "I can't beleef zis iz ze zame horse!" (I could understand Hans being surprised, but he wasn't nearly as surprised as my parents who had absolutely no idea I was even riding, much less competing in the show.)

Rats was retired in 1972. During the previous 18 months he'd had several bad falls with me and as a result, I'd fractured my kneecap and broken my collarbone badly. We never really found out why he started falling; he had simply begun to stand off for no apparent reason. When faced with a double of oxers, he would often paddle the second spread and he was lucky not to bring himself down time and again. In fact, he'd really become unsafe over very big fences and in the Grand Prix competitions; I felt it was wiser to retire him.

Eldorado was also retired in 1972 (he and Ratification lived on happily after their retirement until we were forced to put them down in 1984) and this left a huge gap in my string because both the horses I had been so successful with during the 1960s had suddenly gone into retirement. They left me with some very happy memories though; I recall that in 1966, when Flyridge was in his last competitive year with me, I took him with Eldorado and Ratification to the Derby and Wanderers Shows where between the three of them, they won 13 out of 17 competitions. What rider could ask for more than that?

Eldorado's retirement coincided with my move to the Transvaal and I was lucky that at least I had a couple of medium A Grades to compete. I have always accepted that in this sport, you must take the good with the bad, so although the following year was very lean for me in terms of major competitions won, I had to grin and bear it.

Towards the end of the following year, I was given an imported 17h.1 Hanoverian to jump. He had begun his career with Hans Günter Winkler and had been jumped by Peter Lavor whose uncle bought him from Hans and imported him for his nephew to ride.

This horse was of course Formaat, and I jumped him successfully until 1977. He was good, but a very different horse to the type I was used to. I had always been used to thoroughbreds and I must admit I have always been happier on a smaller horse. I don't really enjoy riding such big horses as Formaat but despite this, we struck up a good partnership and during the four years I rode him, we had several very good wins together.

Two months after Formaat was given to me, I received a telegram from the President of the Washington Horse Show, inviting me to compete in the Ladies Individual International Championship in Washington DC in late October. (I later learned that the invitation had been at the instigation of American Gold Medallist Billy Steinkraus. Billy had seen me riding in South Africa two years previously when he'd been invited to compete at an indoor show in Cape Town.)

You can imagine my excitement when this two-page telegram arrived; naturally, I immediately cabled back an answer of "Delighted to attend."

The necessary arrangements were made and my husband Des and I decided to leave for the USA about four days after the last day of the 1973 Derby so that we could spend a few days in London.

I have had a major back problem for many years and as luck would have it, several days before the Derby my back completely packed up on me while I was jumping a horse at home. I was in such a bad way that I couldn't even bend down and straighten up without help; if I coughed, it felt as though somebody was sticking a knife into my back.

To cut a long story short, I ended up in hospital where I was given a spinal epidural and kept in bed for the next 36 hours. I was then allowed to get up, and I rode very quietly the day before the Derby. The next day I competed, and as recommended by my orthopaedic surgeon, I rode in a back brace through the whole of that Derby. Four days after the competition ended, Des and I flew to the States via London.

Disaster struck when we arrived in London to discover that our luggage had been lost en route: my jacket, my cap, my boots and breeches and everything else that goes with me — lost. I couldn't bear the thought of having to ride at the Washington Show wearing clothes that didn't belong to me. I could visualise myself having to borrow a jacket which probably wouldn't fit me anywhere, not to mention boots which are the most uncomfortable things to wear if they don't fit correctly. I was most relieved when, 24 hours later, the luggage turned up and we flew on to Washington.

Des and I had been invited to stay with the President of the show at his country estate, and Des went hunting, which he thoroughly enjoyed. Then the show began and we had to get down to some serious business.

The show was to run over five nights and the particular Championship I had been invited to compete for was a round robin competition. This meant that five horses had been pooled for the five lady riders invited, and the riders each had a chance to compete on each horse.

The competition was stiff: Kathy Kusner, a previous winner of this particular competition, was riding for the USA, Anne Moore, the top British woman rider in that year, rode for Britain, and Lalla Nova, leading Italian woman rider, rode for Italy. Unfortunately the French leading lady rider was unable to attend the show so Pilar Cepeda Munroe-Wilson from Peru had been invited in her place.

We were given no opportunity to practise on the horses and get to know them: we just got on and rode them for anything from 15 minutes to half an hour before the class. Then we competed.

On the first night I got a horse called Lazer Beam, a typical South African type of horse of about 16 hands who dumped me in the middle of a parallel while I was warming him up for the class. Luckily (particularly as I wasn't wearing the back brace) I didn't hurt my back, but as he dumped me only seconds before I went into the ring, I only had enough time to remount, give him a hard clout, do one more jump and then go in, so I don't think I rode the best of rounds. However, I managed to go clear and get through to the jump-off where I had a fence down to end up third.

The next night I was allotted a rather pretty and chubby-looking grey horse called Sagittarius who was renowned for being quite a bad stopper.

I was determined to do better than on the first night and, as the competition was a speed event, it really lent itself to some hard riding, so I took a good contact and rode him strongly to win with a very fast round.

On the third night, my ride was a rather long and lanky horse called Steve's Poppet who went in a pelham with no martingale. The owner was insistent that he simply wouldn't jump with a martingale, but after trying him over one or two practice fences just before the competition started, I insisted on having a martingale. If my memory serves me correctly I also changed his bit to a snaffle.

Steve's Poppet jumped very well for two clear rounds but we weren't fast enough to win and ended up being placed third.

The fourth and fifth nights I was to have the two best horses: one of them, a horse called Seven Forty Seven, was a big bay American Thoroughbred with a lovely stride and a big jump. I really enjoyed this horse and had two excellent rounds on him to win the competition.

On the last night I had a big, strong, chestnut horse called Katmandu which had originally been bought for the United States team. However, because of slight unsoundness, Katmandu had never managed to crack a position on the team. Although I was looking forward to the ride on him, I was sceptical about his soundness, particularly as Kathy Kusner had jumped him the night before and she had not had a particularly good round on him.

During the afternoon of the day I was to ride Katmandu, I was sitting chatting to George Morris. He asked me what horse I was riding that evening, and when I replied that I was riding Katmandu, he sounded a little perturbed but then went on to say that he was sure the horse would be fine for that night.

Sure enough, that night Katmandu came striding out like a two-year-old and he gave me two wonderful rounds, the second of which was very fast against the clock, and with which I won the competition.

I was thrilled to find that I had won the overall Championship, as I'd had a fourth the first night, a first the second night, then a third and then two firsts. I hoped that I could return the following year to defend my title, but unfortunately the competition was discontinued as were several others, because the show ran so late into the night. The competition only started at about 0h30 so you can imagine that by the time people went home it was well after 2h30 and the day's programme started again the next morning at eight o'clock.

Formaat wins the puissance at the Cape Indoor Show, clearing 6'8" (2,03 m)

It was during this show that I was to pick up some information about how to work Formaat. I sat for several hours during the day watching Hans Winkler working his international horses on the flat and also over fences, and from watching him, I was able to study his technique and put the same sort of work into Formaat. He responded immediately as he had originally been trained by Hans Winkler, and I will go so far as to say that within six weeks Formaat stopped being a careless ox and became careful. He was certainly a horse to contend with in the major competitions: so much so, that it was only several months later that Formaat won the National South African Championship with me in 1974. It just goes to show how important it is that a horse is correctly schooled.

Formaat also won the 1976 Derby for me, and because he was a big and rather slow horse, I was able to compete successfully on him in puissance competitions, many of which he won. It was in fact in a puissance at the Rand Show in 1977 that he banked a wall of 1,98 m and fell on top of me, tearing the ligaments in my left ankle and smashing my collarbone so badly it had to be pinned.

I simply couldn't afford to ride horses that were going to fall with me, especially as this was the second time I'd broken my collarbone badly. I knew that if I injured it again, I might be put out of action for good and as Formaat was then 17 years old, I stopped riding him and suggested he be retired.

6

My Marriage

DES AND I met at a Cape Hunt opening breakfast and I took a liking to him straight away. In those days, he was running a stable in Hout Bay and as I had a young horse for sale, I suggested he should come and see it.

Des turned up to see this horse about a week later and I happened to be holding a party the same evening so I invited him along. We then saw quite a lot of each other over the next five years but, for no particular reason, lost touch completely and didn't see each other again until about 1972. We met again at the Goodwood Show, just a week before I was due to leave the Cape for good to live in Johannesburg. I was holding what was to be my farewell party later that week and I asked Des whether he would like to come. I told him to bring a partner, but when he arrived at the party without one, I was quite pleased.

We spent a lot of time together that evening and the next morning at six o'clock I left for Johannesburg.

Three weeks later Des arrived in Johannesburg. We started to go out again, became engaged at the end of May, and got married on the 8th of September that year.

It was Des who introduced me to Jack Russell terriers: as an engagement present he had given

me a puppy called Barnabus and I adored him, so I was shattered when he was killed by an Alsation on our second wedding anniversary.

Over the following weeks, I missed Barnabus terribly. He'd gone everywhere with me and I didn't know what to do with myself now that he was gone. Then I discovered that his father (Bumble) needed a new home because his owners were emigrating, and I was only too delighted to have him.

Unlike Barnabus, Bumble never travelled to shows with me because he tended to fight with other dogs, but by the time he eventually died of old age, I was so into Jack Russells, I was totally lost without one.

Barnabus and Bumble had been the sturdy, short-legged and muscular type of Jack Russell I like. Many of them are a bit leggy or lacking in substance, so for the next two months I dragged Des around Johannesburg to look at every Jack Russell that was to be found and nothing would please me.

Eventually we heard about a Jack Russell Club Show which was to be held the following Sunday, so off we went, all the way out to Henley-on-Klip, hoping that perhaps we might find another Barnabus or Bumble there.

While I was walking around viewing all the dogs and watching them go through their paces, Des happened to find the one and only puppy that had been brought along to the show because its parents were there and it couldn't be left at home. It was the only one left of the litter and the breeders had decided to keep him for themselves.

I wasn't interested in the puppy because I had decided to find and keep tabs on a good dog and bitch in the hope that I might get a good puppy from them.

Eventually, I found what I was looking for and approached the owners to ask if I could have pick of the litter. I did all this without realising that the male and female were in fact the mother and father of the funny little puppy that Des liked so much.

By this stage I had begun to find the day quite upsetting because so many of the dogs looked like Barnabus or Bumble, so when I found out that the puppy was the offspring of the dog and bitch I liked, I asked Des to find out whether the owners would let us buy him.

Des went to the owners and explained how upset I had been at losing Bumble, and the owners said they were a bit worried about keeping the dog puppy in case he and his father fought when the puppy grew up, so they decided we could have him if we just paid for the inoculations he'd just had.

Boots

I subsequently named the puppy Boots, partly because he had big feet, and partly because Mr Vogel of New York, who specialises in making handmade riding boots, had just visited us in South Africa. His nickname was Boots, and as I'd been buying from him for years, I decided to name my puppy after him.

Boots goes everywhere with me except overseas and to Sun City (he doesn't like Sun City). He can't wait to jump into the horsebox and then he lies on the dashboard for most of the journey. It can't be very comfortable with all the vibration, but he doesn't seem to notice.

Fortunately, he's no worry at shows; he just wanders off and talks to his friends and then comes back to see where I am. He has his own pillow at home and at shows and he sleeps on the bed, even at all the hotels; he's never been turned away yet but I suppose there's always a first time. I even fly him to Cape Town if I have a show there and he travels in his own special box which goes into the pressurised hold. He has to be tranquilised first, which doesn't impress him at all, but he's far less miserable than he would be if we left him at home. When I do have to leave him to go on an overseas trip, he spends just about every minute sitting on the table next to the front door staring out of the window and when I return, he goes absolutely crazy with joy. On the whole, he gives me so much pleasure that a Jack Russell was obviously the perfect engagement present to me; the novelty has never worn off.

7

Honey Girl

I BOUGHT Honey Girl following my accident with Formaat, and it was probably a good thing that I decided to stop riding him because it would have been difficult to combine such different horses: Honey Girl was a thoroughbred standing a mere 16 hands whereas Formaat had been 17h.1in. — and big with it.

I first saw her in 1973 when Eugene du Plessis brought her on a course I regularly gave in Bloemfontein, and I wanted her from the moment I set eyes on her. This was despite the fact that I had long since decided to steer clear of mares (even though I'd had such good mares as Qui Va La) there being no doubt that they are less consistent than a gelding. They do have their off days, and people who compete seriously can't afford to lose competitions as a result. However, the sight of Honey Girl swept all my logical arguments aside because she jumped as though somebody had hidden a trampoline on the takeoff. It was many years before I was to have the opportunity to ride her and find out that she also *felt* as though she was bouncing off a trampoline, and good though Watchfire is, the feel he gives me off the ground and over the jump doesn't compare with jumping Honey Girl. Mind you, I have to admit that Watchfire is much faster against the clock. Still, to this day Honey Girl is the best horse I have ever had.

Left: *Honey Girl displays her extravagant technique*

I asked Eugene for an option on her there and then and when I went home, I wondered how long it would be before he contacted me with an offer to sell — or whether he might never sell her at all — perish the thought!

I gave the course in Bloemfontein every two or three months and when teaching there, I stayed with Dr Piet Coetzee whose daughter, Louisa, was a pupil of mine.

Several months after the first time I saw Honey Girl, Dr Coetzee picked me up from the airport and as he was driving back to his house, he said, "We've just bought a new horse for Louisa, and I'm afraid we might have paid a little too much for it."

Naturally, I was interested to know what he'd bought.

"You probably know the horse — a little brown mare called Honey Girl."

To say that my heart sank can't possibly give any indication of how I felt. I actually felt physically sick and I don't know how I managed to force a smile and say, "What did you pay for her?"

"Two thousand," said Dr Coetzee.

Two thousand! I would have

paid five times more if Eugene had only given me the chance. "You got a bargain," I told him.

"Do you really think so?" he said. And I told him I'd give him a profit on Honey Girl any day, which was when I secured another first option on her.

For the duration of that course, I switched to automatic pilot so that I appeared to be functioning normally but, deep down, I was sick to the bones at having lost the chance to buy her. It was all I could do to face Eugene without hauling him off his horse and beating him to a pulp, but obviously he hadn't done it to upset me purposely. He'd probably simply forgotten I asked for the first option.

After that, I taught Louisa for another four years, during which time she and Honey Girl won a number of major titles, not least of which was the South African Junior Championship in Durban.

I tried on a number of occasions to persuade Dr Coetzee to sell, but he wouldn't, and it was agony to have to watch somebody else ride a horse I wanted so much. The only bright spot in the whole affair was that Louisa was a fair rider; I don't think I could have stood to watch Honey Girl in the hands of someone who couldn't sit one side of a bike.

Louisa and I often attended the same shows, but we didn't compete against each other because she was still in juniors. However, at the 1977 Rand Show, Louisa was competing in the Adult Medium A Grade classes and she qualified for the championship held on the last day of the show.

It was at that show that Formaat and I came to grief in the puissance, and the accident put me out of the show completely. I had been told not to ride for two months. Four days after my admission to hospital, I was discharged so that I could return to the showground to watch the White Horse Whisky Championship.

Because my left leg and right collarbone were affected, it was impossible for me to use crutches. There was nothing else for it but to use a wheelchair and my husband, Des, pushed me into the stands.

When the crowd realised I was there, people started clapping, but it took a few seconds before I realised that this was for me; that these people were applauding me — making it clear that they were glad to see me there — I was very moved.

The White Horse Whisky Championship was a damn good competition that year, but one thing stands out in my mind: I watched Anneli Wucherpfennig (*née* Drummond-Hay) ride an incredibly fast and accurate round on Seville, a brilliant horse I knew had been sired by Jerez who, in turn, had been sired by Dramatic. I knew also that Honey Girl was by Arctic Circle, by Dramatic, and as a matter of interest, Watchfire's sire is a full brother to Seville, so he is a great-grandson of Dramatic.

That decided me. If it killed me, I was going to have Honey Girl and, as though it was a matter of life and death, I turned to Des and told him so.

"Oh yes?" he said bluntly. "And what are you going to buy her with?"

I had about R5 000 in my savings account at the time, but that would hardly have been enough to put a deposit on her tail (which, incidentally, has never grown longer than the top of her hocks to this day). "I don't know," I told him, "but I'm going to see Dr Coetzee right now, and I'm going to buy her. Are you coming?"

Des thought that perhaps the fall had unhinged me. "You're wasting your time," he pointed out. "He'll never sell and even if he did, you haven't got the money to buy her."

Not to be deterred, I turned to Arina Devenish who was working for me at the time (and who later became the wife of Eugene du Plessis). "Will you give me a push?" I said, and an hour later, her car drew up outside Dr Coetzee's.

It was pouring with rain and instead of bothering with the wheelchair (which we'd folded up and put in the boot of the car), I hobbled, hopped and practically dragged myself to the front door of the house where the Coetzees were staying.

He was quite surprised to see me, particularly as I was in such a state of disrepair at the time, but he invited me in and listened politely while I explained that I just had to have Honey Girl, come what may. I begged him, pleaded with him, and promised him the most outrageous sum if he would only at least consider selling Honey Girl, so he said, "What sort of outrageous sum?" And I offered him R15 000 in cash (I didn't have anything like R15 000; nor did I have the faintest idea how I was going to get it, should he agree), and I also offered him a good young horse worth R3 000.

I finally left with Arina after Dr Coetzee agreed to at least think about selling Honey Girl. The following day, he phoned me. I won't say I was confident he would sell her, but I was certainly hopeful — it was, after all, a great deal of money to turn down, but he said he'd decided to reject my kind offer.

I replaced the receiver and slumped deeper into my wheelchair. OK, if he wouldn't sell for that, I'd up the price. I phoned him back. "I'll give you fifteen thousand, plus the young horse worth three thousand, plus a B Grade showjumper called Super V. He's got to be worth ten thousand.

Dr Coetzee paused for thought. He knew Super V, a previously top-class horse who had sprung a hock 18 months before. Although now sound and jumping B Grade courses once more, Super V didn't quite lift that hind leg as he should, which meant that his future as an international A Grade would probably be impaired. He would, however, be good enough to win plenty of the Adult Medium A Grade competitions once he'd accumulated enough B Grade points to enable him to upgrade again, and he had the advantage of being an extremely experienced (if rather hot) horse.

Furthermore, Louisa had already started university and I pointed out to Dr Coetzee that she could no longer do Honey Girl justice. I said, "If Louisa takes Super V, she'll still have a good horse; she'll still be able to get onto the Orange Free State Senior Team, and she'll still have a lot of fun. What do you say?"

Dr Coetzee said, "I'll think about it."

And that was my best shot. I knew there was nothing more I could offer, so I tried to push Honey Girl out of my mind.

The following weekend I went down to Pietermaritzburg for the Royal Show. I wasn't riding because I was still incapacitated, but Louisa was there with Honey Girl and I asked Dr Coetzee whether he'd made his mind up yet.

He hadn't, but on the last day of the show, he agreed to allow me to have Honey Girl vetted back in Johannesburg, and I thought that was an extremely hopeful sign.

Dr Coetzee was staying with friends in Johannesburg and Honey Girl was being stabled there. I was on the spot when Dr Azzie examined her on the Sunday and you can imagine my relief when he gave her the all clear.

Dr Coetzee, having allowed me to have her vetted, surely couldn't say he wasn't prepared to sell . . . could he?

I couldn't believe my ears when he told me that he still hadn't made up his mind; that the answer might yet be no; that I'd have to give him more time to think. I could see Honey Girl slipping away from me when he trucked her home to Bloemfontein the next day.

You know, Honey Girl has always got to me. People say that they love a particular horse, often meaning that they're pretty fond of it. What I felt for Honey Girl was indescribable; we had an almost telepathic bond, and I have never felt that way for any other horse before or since. I couldn't bear the thought of not having her and I wondered what I was going to do about it if Dr Coetzee finally turned me down.

The day after he took Honey Girl back to Bloemfontein, Dr Coetzee phoned me. I was sitting in the living room at the time, trying to come to terms with the fact that I'd probably lost her. As I picked up the receiver, I wondered who could be phoning me at ten o'clock at night, and my heart skipped a beat when I heard Dr Coetzee's voice. "Gonda," he said, "you can have Honey Girl."

What did I do? Did I leap round the room whooping at the top of my voice? No, I burst into tears. Totally unable to speak, I handed the phone to Des, who had no sooner replaced the receiver than he went out into the yard and loaded up Super V and the young horse. "I'm going to pick her up," he said, "before Dr Coetzee changes his mind!" Even today as I write this, it brings a lump to my throat. No human or animal has ever had the effect on me that Honey Girl has. I couldn't believe she was finally mine and I kept expecting something to snatch her away from me at the last minute. It wasn't until Des arrived back from Bloemfontein with the lorry that I dared hope I really had her.

Then, the box rolled into the yard and Des jumped down from the cab, his face the picture of misery. "Gonda," he said. "I don't know how I'm going to tell you this . . ."

Please God, I thought. Don't tell me Des got there and Dr Coetzee said no.

"What?" I shouted. "What went wrong?"

Des grinned. "Nothing," he said. "She's in the lorry."

I didn't know whether to kiss him or kill him!

In all the years I'd wanted her, I'd never even had the chance to sit on Honey Girl. I badly wanted to get her going as soon as possible, but I happened to buy her the week before I left for England as part of the 1977 unofficial South African team.

I was still suffering slightly with the injuries I'd received after Formaat and I fell, but the doctor had given me permission to get back into the saddle. Honey Girl felt as though she was jumping off a trampoline. In fact, she felt better than I had ever imagined she would, and I couldn't wait to get the trip over with so that I could start working her properly.

The first major show I took her to was the Pretoria Agricultural Show in August. I entered her for the Medium A Grade classes because that was as much as she had ever done, but on the last day, I jumped her in the International Accumulator, which she won.

Honey Girl then went on to qualify for the Derby in October 1977. However, she had 16 faults by the time we'd got as far as the stile (which was the 13th fence) so I retired her as it was clear that she wasn't really ready to compete in the Derby.

Several days later, she was slightly sore and we suspected that she'd jarred her side bone. She had to be rested until January, after which she was jumped at the Rand Show in April. Once again, I put her into the medium A Grade classes.

Honey Girl had been ineligible to compete in the Grand Prix because I had only entered her in the medium classes. However, it so happened that she had qualified by default for the Star of Star competition because the horse that had qualified before her had been injured and couldn't compete. I was therefore allowed to jump her in that class where she came second, a placing that qualified her for the Rand Show Championship, which she went on to win.

Honey Girl then went from strength to strength and when I entered her for the 1978 Derby, she tied for second place with my other horse, Country Cottage.

In 1979 she won the Derby with the only clear and then went on to win the SA Championship and the Varig Airlines Championship, which won me a trip for two to Rio. She was also runner-up in the first ever FEI World Cup where she was 27 seconds faster than the winner's time, only to have the third last fence down, giving us four faults. Nevertheless, it was quite an achievement for a little mare.

Then, as it does from time to time, disaster struck. On our return from South America, it was found that Honey Girl had jarred both sesamoids in front as a result of a groom's mishandling her in the yard. The same groom was also responsible for Country Cottage losing an eye during our absence, and needless to say, we sacked him on the spot. That wasn't much help to me though. My two best horses were in a terrible state, and anyone who runs a yard will know what it feels like to be away from home wondering what the hell's going on while you're not there, only to return to find your worst fears confirmed.

Honey Girl was out of action for eight months and, to bring her back into work, we swam her at a veterinary hospital in Alberton for five weeks. Then she had only ten days' work before the 1980 FEI where she was runner-up to Mickey Louw riding Epol Appraise. Honey Girl then won the Derby and straight after the Derby, Mickey and I went to Bern in Switzerland for the presentation of the FEI World Cup awards.

The day after the presentation, I caught the first plane back to South Africa, arriving only an hour before the first qualifying class for the South African Grand Prix. The results in this class and two others made Honey Girl the highest qualifier for the Grand Prix, which she won.

By winning that competition, she made me the only ever outright winner of the Grand Slam, for I had been lucky enough to win the SA Championship, the SA Grand Prix and the SA Derby all in the same year.

Then misfortune decided to rear its head yet again: while I was competing at the 1981 Cape Protea Show, Honey Girl suffered a bad injury.

The competition was an Accumulator, and Mickey Louw was leading before I entered the arena. The atmosphere was absolutely electric and I knew that Honey Girl was probably the only horse in the competition who had the slightest chance of beating Mickey's time.

I knew that we had put in a terrifically fast round as we approached the second to last jump, but I didn't know whether it was fast enough to win. Consequently, as soon as we landed, I turned Honey Girl very sharp into the last in the hope of knocking off a second.

Honey Girl backed off the fence

(an oxer) and jumped very high, catching the back pole with her left hind leg as she landed. I knew within a second of landing that something terrible had happened to her and when I leapt off and saw the hind leg dangling uselessly, my first reaction was to think she'd broken it.

There is no point in even attempting to explain how I felt as I stood in the arena and looked at that leg. Nothing I say can possibly convey what was going through my mind; I thought Honey Girl was finished, and the crowd seemed to echo my thoughts as the entire stand fell absolutely silent.

Some seconds later, I managed to pull myself together sufficiently to lead her gently out of the arena; then I stood aside as a vet examined her. I was waiting for him to tell me what I thought I already knew — that he'd have to put her down — so I was almost relieved when he told me she'd torn the fibularus tertius tendon, even though that was a serious injury.

I must add here that the accident has had a definite effect on me subconsciously. Even now, years later, I won't take the chance of turning a horse so sharply. Instead of two strides, I take three, instead of three seconds, I take four: it has definitely slowed me down that fraction because at the back of my mind, I remember what happened to Honey Girl.

There was no question of travelling Honey Girl back to Johannesburg in the state she was in, so I flew my vet down from Johannesburg and we took Honey Girl to Judy Stegeman, a friend of mine who has stables in Cape Town.

André explained that in order for the tendon to have any chance whatsoever of healing, we had to render Honey Girl utterly immobile, so for two months, she stood in a crush that had been erected in one of the stables. For a thoroughbred, she bore it all with great fortitude, but careful feeding and massage, plus a groom who slept in the box at night with her, saw her through.

The crush was to be dismantled after two months so that Honey Girl could at least walk around the stable, and we would know then whether there was any chance at all of her making a complete recovery.

I smoked quite a bit in those days — 20 cigarettes a day if not more — and I remember that when I made the journey from Johannesburg to the Cape to see what would happen when the crush was taken down, I made a pact with myself that if Honey Girl could walk, I'd give up smoking.

I remember standing by the stable door as the last poles of the crush were taken out by a groom, and when Honey Girl took first one unsteady step, and then another. I sat on the manger watching her and I smoked my last cigarette ever.

Honey Girl spent another two months in the stable, after which she was led out in hand twice a day for a month. Then she came home to rest in a paddock which had been specially constructed for her and was extremely small so that she couldn't fresh and jump around; the last thing we wanted her to do was to damage the ligament again.

Three months later, we decided it was safe for her to be allowed into a larger area, and after six months in the big paddock, I brought her back into light work. However, after three months of light work it became clear that Honey Girl wasn't carrying herself properly on a left-handed circle and the vet recommended that we pin fire her. This meant that she was to be out of work for another four months and I was beginning to wonder whether I'd ever ride her again. In fact, it was February 1983 before she was fit enough to

Honey Girl forces me at the last jump in the 1978 Derby

compete once more, and the first show I entered her for happened to be at the Cape Protea where she had injured herself two years before.

Just as I was about to ride her into the main arena, a steward approached me and said, "Would you mind walking and trotting her around the arena for a minute before the bell? There's going to be an announcement."

I wondered what was going on until, as I entered the arena, the band started to play "Land of Hope and Glory" and the crowd gave Honey Girl a standing ovation. It was very moving because it wasn't only the crowd who had wondered whether they'd ever see Honey Girl in the arena again: I'd had my doubts — believe me.

Honey Girl was almost back to her usual form and she gave me a second in the Grand Prix and a second in the Championship. However, she didn't qualify for the Rand Show because she'd been out of work and hadn't accumulated any points before the closing date of entry to enable her to compete. It seemed harsh to me at the time, especially when she was so obviously capable of competing, but rules are rules and I just had to put up with it.

Honey Girl then went on to win the Pietermaritzburg Grand Prix, but bad luck hadn't finished with us yet: the day after the Grand Prix, as I was warming her up for the Championship, she suddenly went lame.

This time it was a small splint

causing the trouble and after the vet removed it, I managed to get her fit in time for the Derby.

The first and second day of the Derby passed uneventfully enough and after competing we loaded Honey Girl up and drove her home. When we lowered the ramp and started to unload her, she jumped to one side and slipped off the ramp. As a result, she cut her left hind leg which needed a few stitches and that put an end to my competing on her in the Derby. However, I wasn't worried about the injury itself: the thought at the back of my mind was that at least it wasn't something serious that had put her out of action. It was only some weeks later, when she was still lame on that hind leg, that I asked the vet to take a closer look.

That was when he gave me the devastating news that in slipping from the ramp, Honey Girl had damaged the tendon again. To give it sufficient time to heal would have meant giving her another three to six months off, maybe even longer, and Honey Girl was already 15 years old.

As I listened to what the vet was saying, it seemed to me that time almost stood still. I thought of all the things she'd done for me and of everything she meant to me, and I knew that I couldn't go on like this. I felt that with so many omens telling me not to jump her any more, I ought to pay heed and stop. It's always tempting to battle on with an exceptionally good horse, but there comes a point when you've just got to see sense about the situation, so I retired her.

We hoped to breed from her and sent her to John and Greg Cleverdon, but Honey Girl wouldn't even look at the aristocratic husbands we chose, so we eventually ran her with a teaser. The plan was that after one foal by the teaser, she'd get the general idea and we could send her back to members of the aristocracy. However, Honey Girl decided that one foal was quite enough thank you. She was a career lady, not a housewife, and she could see no way of combining the two occupations. Her filly, Honey Lass, is a four-year-old now, but it doesn't look as though she's going to follow in her mother's footsteps. She's going to be too small for a start, but notwithstanding that, she shows a promising jump and she'll probably make a good horse for a junior someday.

Honey Girl now lives in the 1 ha paddock here at home, as fat and as cheeky as ever. She's very jealous of her paddock; or is it that she's jealous of me riding anything else, I wonder, because when I take another horse in there to jump, she charges at us with her ears flat back. It's almost as though she's saying, "What are you doing up there? You should be riding me!"

I often wish I could be doing just that.

Honey Girl in retirement

8

Country Cottage and Isis Bridge

AT THE same time as I bought Honey Girl, I bought two other first-class horses: Country Cottage, who was to jump alongside Honey Girl, and Isis Bridge, who was to take over when Country Cottage and Honey Girl retired.

Both Cottage and Isis Bridge were by the same sire, Initial. Cottage was a pitch-black horse and Isis a beautiful grey.

Country Cottage, an ex-Zimbabwean horse, had belonged to Yvonne Magner, one of Zimbabwe's leading riders. Yvonne was a good friend of mine and when she and her husband moved to Johannesburg, they came to visit me one Saturday afternoon.

Naturally, I showed them around the stable yard and while they were looking at my horses, I happened to mention that my B Grade (who at that time was a horse called Pepper King) had just gone down with biliary. This was a great disappointment to me as I was leaving on Monday for the Kimberley and Bloemfontein shows, and without Pepper King, I wouldn't have a B Grade to travel with me.

When Yvonne heard this, she immediately said, "Our new B Grade is down here. Perhaps you'd like to take him with you?"

Yvonne's new B Grade was, of course, Country Cottage, and I had heard that he had an exceptionally good jump, so I took her up on the offer.

Country Cottage

Within two hours I had ridden and jumped Cottage and I liked him very much. So the decision was made that he would stay with me and go to those shows in place of Pepper King.

That evening we all went out to dinner and, during dinner, I asked Yvonne for a first option on Cottage.

Although she couldn't foresee ever wanting to sell him, Yvonne agreed and I secured the option there and then by putting it in writing on a small piece of paper.

The following day I took him to Bloemfontein and Kimberley where he cleaned up by winning three out of the three B Grade classes at Kimberley, which gave him the Victor Ludorum, and three out of the four B Grade classes at Bloemfontein, which again gave him the Victor Ludorum and also meant that he was now one point off A Grade.

Then, on his return from the shows, he fell ill with travelling sickness, a form of pneumonia, within two hours of arriving back at my stables. I will never forget that day. My telephone was out of order; I was due to fetch a friend I hadn't seen for ten years from the airport, and Cottage arrived back looking very off colour. By the time I had managed to get the vet, the horse really was ill and was standing in the box with his head hanging down and shaking like a leaf.

The vet did the right thing by giving him the usual injections, but unfortunately it turned out that Cottage was allergic to one of them and through this injection we nearly lost him. You can imagine how I felt at this time, having somebody else's horse totally my responsibility, a very valuable horse, a potential top A Grade showjumper, who was standing there quietly dying on me.

The vet kept him going on adrenalin injections. By this time, my grooms were virtually holding Cottage up. He was swaying and threatening to fall, soaked with sweat, when the vet came upon a lung clearing injection, which proved to be the turning point. Had the vet not tried it as a last resort, we would definitely have lost Cottage. When I realised he was going to pull through, the relief was absolutely enormous. I don't know what I would have done if he'd died, particularly as he belonged to someone else.

Five and a half hours later, my friend Di was collected at the airport wondering what on earth had happened because of course with my phone out of order there was no way she could contact me, nor could I leave any message for her. In those days, I didn't have neighbours with a phone and there was no way I was going to leave Cottage. Fortunately, she was very understanding when she found out what had happened.

For the following three weeks, I kept Cottage at home and nursed him until the vet gave him the all clear, and then, of course, he went back to Yvonne.

During this time I had tried to buy him from her but she said that she wasn't interested in selling; she wanted to compete him in A Grade as soon as possible. Once he was fit again, Yvonne took him to the Chrysler Classics Show where she won the B Grade Championship, which made him A Grade.

Then, three months later, Yvonne approached me at the Pretoria Agricultural Show and said that due to the move from Zimbabwe and financial pressure, she had to sell Cottage. It was good news for me, of course, but I couldn't help feeling sorry for Yvonne who had obviously thought of every possible way of keeping him.

I immediately said that I wanted him, but that I couldn't buy him without borrowing the money from a friend in Cape Town and I knew that it wouldn't be fair to keep her on a string, so I said, "Look, I have the written option on the horse but I can't stop you from letting other people see him. By all means, let them see him, but make it clear that if I manage to raise the money to buy him, I have first option."

Yvonne agreed to this and some ten days later, Sue Louw, then wife of Springbok Showjumper Mickey Louw, arrived at my house for lunch. During lunch, she happened to mention that she'd heard Cottage had been sold to Anneli and Errol Wucherpfennig. If I had a mouthful of food at the time, I'm only surprised I didn't choke on it. I got up immediately, went to the phone and phoned Yvonne to ask her if this was true. "Oh yes," she said. "I sold him yesterday. In fact, Anneli's coming to fetch him in about an hour's time."

"But Yvonne," I said. "you can't do this. I have a written option on the horse."

"But you told me that you didn't have the money to buy him," said Yvonne.

"True," I replied, "but at the

same time, I told you I was trying to raise the money and I thought I made it clear to you that you should tell people so. I also expected you to come back to me before you made any final decision in case I had been able to raise the money." Then I put the phone down and wrote out a cheque before getting into the car and driving to Yvonne's like a bat out of hell.

By this time, Anneli had arrived to fetch the horse. She had given a cheque to Yvonne, but when I arrived with my cheque I *insisted* on Yvonne taking it and I then told Anneli that she couldn't remove the horse.

"Why not?"

"Because I had first option, in writing, and I've just given a cheque for him, so he's mine."

Anneli didn't really know what was going on. She was naturally very upset and phoned her husband, so I phoned my husband, Yvonne phoned her husband, and of course there was general chaos all round. We all subsequently phoned our lawyers and Cottage stayed in his stable at the Magners'. Des and I then spent until midnight with my lawyer who arranged a court interdict to prevent anyone from moving Cottage from the Magners' property — and there he stayed.

The next morning at 6h30, Yvonne's husband phoned me to say that if my cheque was met at the bank when it opened that morning, the horse was mine. If, however, the cheque wasn't met, Cottage would go to the Wucherpfennigs. The reason he said this was that when I gave Yvonne the cheque the day before, I asked her not to bank it for two days as the money I had borrowed from Cape Town hadn't yet been transferred to my account. So, at 8h30 that morning, my mother and I stood outside the doors of my bank in Sandton City, and as it opened, we went in to see the bank manager. My mother stood surety for me — and Country Cottage was mine.

It was all very unfortunate: somewhere along the line, there had been a total misunderstanding, but as I had the written option, there was no way the horse could actually be sold to anybody else.

Anneli was obviously upset and disappointed at having lost the horse, but I'm glad to say that we didn't end up not on speaking terms, and we remained friends.

Cottage went on to be very successful with me, but unfortunately for him, I owned him at the same time as Honey Girl and she totally overshadowed him. There were many occasions when he in fact beat Honey Girl, but people always raved about her, never him. The two of them fought out many a major competition coming first and second, and in their last year of competing together, Honey Girl won the Showjumper of the Year Award with Cottage taking second place only two points behind her.

Incidentally, Cottage was very similar to Watchfire in looks: although Cottage was a much bigger horse, he was also black.

Unlike his brother, Isis Bridge was the living proof that looks are skin deep. He was an absolute terror to ride and to handle, and he had been sent from Zimbabwe for me to sell because he was too well known in Zimbabwe for anybody in their right mind to want to buy him. He had a reputation for being a confirmed stopper, and had been eliminated from his last 15 shows where he had competed in junior D Grade.

Despite all that, I liked Isis Bridge from the word go, but I wasn't under any illusions; I knew that he had a mind of his own and after trying unsuccessfully to sell him, I took a chance and bought him myself for R1 250.

Isis Bridge

After a lot of hard work was put into him, Isis Bridge then proceeded to shoot through C Grade gaining over 100 points in a year. He also did well in B Grade and then settled nicely into A Grade, but he was very much my second string horse and I had Honey Girl and Country Cottage in the major classes.

Mickey Louw once tried to buy him from me and as this happened to coincide with Isis Bridge going through a stage of being even more horrible than usual, I was tempted to sell. Thank goodness I didn't, for he was to take over from Country Cottage and Honey Girl when they were retired in the early eighties.

I think I can honestly say that Isis Bridge was one of the most difficult horses I have ever had. When he arrived, he couldn't be trusted in the stable as he was a bad kicker; he would also bite, given half a chance. I have to admit that to his dying day I never once turned my back on him in the box, for if anyone were to do so, he snaked after them from behind.

He managed to get me one day: I'd ducked under the rails of his paddock to adjust his fly fringe. Even as I did so, I wondered whether I was being wise: my right arm was strapped to my body because of an accident I'd had some weeks before. Isis Bridge obviously sensed my lack of confidence and he took the opportunity to have a real *go* by rearing up to his full height, lunging at me with his teeth bared, and coming down on the top of my head.

Fortunately, as he did so, he pushed me back through the single-rail paddock fence and I have often wondered whether he'd have had another go if that fence hadn't been there. In the event, the fence saved me and I ended up with a cut to my head which needed five stitches, but the experience gave me a hell of a shock and I've never fogotten it.

Isis Bridge took a tremendous amount of work and I remember that prior to his winning the South African Championship for me in 1980, I'd spent an hour working him in because he was giving me an argument about an ice-cream boy with an ice-cream cart that he didn't want to go past. I was pretty tired at the end of this session and Isis Bridge was sweating all over, so I really didn't rate my chances of winning the Championship that year as I thought I'd worn him out.

Isis Bridge, however, had amazing stamina, and I think I can go so far as to say he proceeded to give me the best three rounds he had ever jumped in his entire life.

To look at him, you wouldn't think that butter could melt in his mouth, for he was the perfect con artist. You could work him for ten minutes and think that everything was 100%, that all the work had been done and that he was now ready for the competition ahead. Then he would blow completely, spook at everything, not concentrate, and be utterly impossible in the ring. Eventually I came to the conclusion that if I worked him terribly hard before a competition and then gave him about half an hour's breather, this was my only hope of getting any sense out of him. He honestly seemed to thrive on work, and although I hated having arguments with him, it seemed to be the only answer in the long run. This is something I try to steer clear of with my horses as arguing often does more harm than good. Both Isis and Cottage had frequent arguments with me and I sometimes wondered whether they'd inherited this streak from their sire.

In the six years that Isis Bridge was an A Grade he always seemed to be dogged by bad luck for the Derby and he only competed in it twice. The first year in which he managed to compete, he was the highest qualifier but, as we entered the arena, the heavens opened — and when I say opened, I really mean opened. He was courageous and went around the course, but we ended up with a total of 16 faults.

Then he developed a type of blood disorder as a result of which he came down with laminitis twice in two years. He also began to have a problem with a stomach muscle which every now and again he would pull, not necessarily when jumping a big jump — you could in fact be trotting over a cross pole when this would happen.

The year after he took 16 faults at the Derby I entered him for the Derby Show again, but I had to withdraw because of either the pulled stomach muscle or laminitis, I can't remember which. Then, in 1985, he won the Derby in a jump-off between Barry Taylor and the late Lochlan McLochlan.

This was to be his last ever success for, tragically in January 1986 I lost Isis Bridge. Two vets spent the entire night trying to save him, but in the early hours of the morning, we had to admit defeat when we discovered that he had an internal rupture, and we put him down.

9

Flaunt and Watchfire

AFTER losing Isis Bridge, I was again without a top horse as my other two horses, Flaunt and All the Aces, were medium A Grades at that time. This meant that I wasn't going to have a ride in the 1986 Rand Show which was coming up three months later.

Flaunt had been given to me a few years earlier by a friend of mine, Peter Wright. Like his father before him, Peter was a racehorse breeder. Many years earlier, his father had bred and raced a horse called Royal Affair, which was the first horse ever to be exported from this country for racing in America.

Peter gave Flaunt to me as a result of our bumping into each other at the Cape Protea Show. I'd gone up to the grounds early one morning to watch a competition, and I found Peter sitting in the stand. It was quite a pleasant surprise to bump into him again and after we'd greeted each other, Peter grinned and said, "How would you like a nice horse?"

I grinned back and replied, "I'd love one. Tell me about it," so he told me that the horse was Flaunt, a three-year-old that Peter intended to race until the end of the year. "He's a colt at the moment," said Peter, "But I intend to geld him, especially as he doesn't show too much promise as a racehorse. He's won a couple of races though and I'm hoping he'll win me one or two more before the year's out."

"Where is he?" I asked, and Peter said he was with Leslie Cawcutt in Milnerton. "Go and have a look at him. If you like him, tell me, and when he's finished his racing career later this year, I'll give you a ring."

A couple of days later, Des and I went to see Flaunt; a long, tall, very narrow, pretty ugly, skinny-looking horse.

"Well," said Des. "He is a *gift* I suppose."

I studied Flaunt further and came to the conclusion that he had rather a nice head. "I like him," I said, and I decided to take him and see what would happen.

The following November, Peter phoned me to say that Flaunt had now finished racing and that if I wanted him, I could take him. "Pay for his trucking to Johannesburg," he said, "and he's all yours to keep, to sell, to do whatever you like with."

At that time, Des was involved with a riding school in Halfway House and, as I had no great hope that Flaunt would make a show-jumper, I trucked him back to Johannesburg with the idea that I would ride him a little and see what he was like before perhaps giving him to Des for the riding

school. Then, after resting him for several days, I got onto him. He was still the skinny, slab-sided, rather ugly long-legged horse we had first seen some months before, but I rapidly discovered that he was perfectly capable of striking off on either leg and of maintaining a nicely balanced canter, although he held his head fairly high and wouldn't keep an even contact at all.

After about five minutes' exercise I trotted him into a little pole which he went straight over, and then into a cross pole which was eventually raised to a height of about 83 cm.

From the first time I put him at the cross pole, Flaunt showed an unbelievably good jump and I laughed and said to Des, "It's into the paddock with him for three months; and there's no chance of you getting him I'm afraid."

Flaunt over the water jump in Cape Town

Flaunt was then turned out in the day and stabled at night. During a three-month rest period he was well fed; he put on condition and started to improve in looks. Today, although his conformation leaves a lot to be desired, he is one of the most beautiful horses in the ring: his coat a fiery red chestnut. He is a horse with tremendous presence who can't resist showing off.

Flaunt soon proved himself to be a quick learner; he's intelligent and went through the grades with no difficulty whatsoever, appearing to find everything easy. He turned A Grade in mid-1982, only three and a half years after I got him, and that's quite an achievement.

Flaunt always had a minor wind problem which caused him to make a slight noise, and this worried me. I wondered whether he would have problems once he started to face the really big competitions, so after he'd had six or seven medium A Grade shows, I decided to have him undergo a wind operation. This was done at the end of the year and put him out for a couple of months.

Unfortunately, he was no sooner back in work than he pulled a small ligament while practising for the Cape Protea Show, so he missed the show and had yet another three months' rest.

As if this weren't irritating enough, just before he was about to be brought back into serious work, he got a fright while being led in from the lunging arena. This caused him to slip and fall over backwards; as a result, he injured his withers so badly he was out of work for another seven months. He then came back into work for three and a half months and I decided to take him down to the Cape Protea Show to jump him in the medium A Grade classes. It was now 1984 and during that show Isis Bridge, who was my top horse, pulled a stomach muscle during a competition prior to the Grand Prix.

This meant that I had no ride for the Grand Prix and Willie Peters (a former A Grade showjumper who is now a top racehorse trainer) suggested I ride Flaunt.

Flaunt had not competed in any A Grade shows for a year, so with tongue in cheek I entered him and nursed him around the course. He went into the jump-off and after I nursed him around that as well, he ended up with a fourth, with which I was very pleased.

The next day Flaunt was competing in the Western Province A Grade Championship and at the second last jump in the jump-off, he threw his head up about two strides in front of the jump. As a result, we misjudged the take-off and he jumped into the obstacle. He didn't fall, but we had quite a nasty crash. However, he appeared to be perfectly sound both for the remainder of the competition and for the days following his return home, but after three weeks' work, he went sore. It took us two months to find out what was wrong with him. The vet diagnosed that Flaunt had torn a splint bone from the right cannon bone, and advised that we pin fire him — which put Flaunt out of work for another five months.

Then it was my turn to be out of action for, some months later, in September, I injured my collarbone again: I was riding a young horse belonging to a pupil of mine at a training show at Carlswold. In the jump-off in the 1,14 m class he stopped, very suddenly, at the first jump, almost overbalancing into the jump with his head and neck over the pole. I slid down his neck, landing flat on my face in the sand paddock and I knew immediately that I'd broken my nose because I felt it crumple. I rolled over onto my back and the horse, which had never regained his balance, proceeded to half fall on, half trample the jump, and he mowed over me, snapping my collarbone with one of his hind feet.

As I sat up, clutching my right shoulder with my left hand, Janie Myburg and my husband, Des, ran to me. With my head bent down, I mumbled, "I'm bleeding." "Yes," said Des, "your nose is bleeding; you must lie back."

"No," I said. "I'm bleeding from my shoulder somewhere." I could feel this awful hot sticky feeling, like coffee running down my chest, and my lap was slowly filling up with a pool of blood. Des removed my hand from my shoulder and the blood began to spurt out, so he found a pressure point and stopped the bleeding.

It was pretty obvious that my collarbone was broken and that there was other damage. A couple of hours later, when I was on the operating table, the surgeon found that the collarbone had punctured the subclavian artery, the main artery to the right arm. Had the collarbone not pierced the skin and had I not bled externally, I might not be here now to tell the tale.

Four hours later, I had a repaired artery and a collarbone that was plated — not too securely — as it was impossible to remove the pin embedded in the collarbone from the accident I'd had with Formaat in 1977. The collarbone had broken at the edge of that pin, very close to my neck, which meant that the screws through the plate could not be properly secured through the collarbone.

As a result of all this, I was strapped up and totally out of action for eight weeks. At the end of November, my third X-rays revealed a non-union; the collarbone had not healed and what's more, it didn't look like it would heal.

At that point, I went to an orthopaedic surgeon who was a good friend of mine. He'd happened to be away at the time of the accident, and when I saw him, I was almost in tears as I said, "You *have* to do something with my collarbone. I must ride at the Rand Show at the end of March."

The surgeon put me back into hospital and took a piece of bone from my right hip which he then grafted onto three sides of my collarbone. He had done this as a last resort and I knew that if it didn't work I'd never ride competitively again. Nobody had given me any great hope that my collarbone would ever mend so I sank into depression. This was an entirely new and strange feeling to me. I'd never been truly depressed before and I didn't know how to handle it.

During this time a top rider, who I'm sure had my best interests at heart, suggested that the time had come for me to retire, especially as I was still at the top.

I gave this a lot of thought, but it made my depression even worse, so I decided that even if I never won another class, providing I didn't make a complete fool of myself, I would continue to do what I love so much.

Three months later, at the beginning of March, my final X-rays still showed non-union of the collarbone, and by this stage I was so depressed that when I walked into the surgeon's room with Des, I was on the verge of a breakdown.

I think the surgeon knew this, and after looking at the X-rays he said, "When you leave here, you can get on a horse."

I couldn't believe my ears as he went on to explain that although the collarbone still hadn't knitted, the graft had taken and to this day, I have no idea whether the collarbone ever did knit. Nor do I care; I have full use of it — and that's good enough for me!

Within days of the surgeon giving me the okay, I was riding four horses a day and I'll never forget getting back on a horse for the first time. In all my life, I'd never been laid off from riding for more than a couple of weeks and now, after being out of the saddle for almost six months, I realised why someone riding for the first time might be frightened: I couldn't believe the distance to the ground!

Three weeks later I competed at the Rand Show, only to be beaten in the Championship by Barry Taylor who pipped me into second place by a tenth of a second.

I was lucky not to be put out of action for good, and because I know that, I no longer take risks by riding stoppers or unsafe horses. Perhaps 15 years ago such a horse might have been a challenge to me, but at 46 I know that if I want to remain competitively at the top, I must have full confidence in my horse. For this reason

I am very careful in the type of horse I choose to ride. Owing to my last collarbone injury, I can't afford to take the chance of a bad accident, although of course accidents will sometimes happen no matter what you do. The thing is, when one is in one's twenties, the confidence lost through a bad accident can often be regained, but that isn't the case as one grows older.

Nevertheless, I was 41 when I had the accident that smashed my collarbone and punctured the main artery to my right arm and, after two operations, a steel plate, a bone graft and six months out of the saddle, I managed to hold my own on Isis Bridge in the Rand Show Championship. This proved to me that I hadn't lost my nerve. But for several months I didn't ride any novice horses because that sort of injury takes many months to heal well enough to take the strain of the sport without causing further damage to the injury. Also, when a specialist tells a woman she's okay and that she can go out and lead a normal life, he doesn't usually expect her to deal with anything heavier than a washing-up bowl or a toddler. It's quite another thing to half halt a strong novice who may not want to listen and may not want to come back to hand.

By the beginning of 1985 Flaunt was sound again and at the Royal Show in Pietermaritzburg he won the Victor Ludorum in the medium classes. Then, just before the Derby, he tore the splint bone from the cannon bone of his *other* leg, and once again we pin fired him; he was out of work for five months. I began to wonder whether our streak of bad luck would ever end.

When he came back into work again, I took him to the Rand Show. As a result of all the injuries, he'd only competed in ten A Grade competitions during the previous three years, so I was determined to nurse him around the international classes. Despite my being so cautious, he was placed in every class and gained a fifth and a sixth in the Grand Prix and the Championship.

All the Aces

For the rest of 1986, I took it very carefully with Flaunt along with a young horse, All the Aces, that had just come through into the big classes. I had bought him as a newly upgraded B Grade some two years earlier. As both Flaunt and All the Aces were new to the big classes, I knew that for 1986 I would have to just coast along quietly. I wanted to give the horses confidence in the big classes, which meant that I couldn't really try to win any first prizes, but as it has always been my policy to look to the future rather than the present, I was quite happy not to ask any questions but to take placings if necessary.

Despite this policy, All the Aces came fourth in the Derby with 12 faults. This was quite an achievement for a horse that had never competed in the Derby before, and he kept up the good work by being runner-up to Flaunt in the 1987 Cape Protea Grand Prix at the Cape Town Show the following year.

By this time, I had started to put pressure on Flaunt, but he coped wonderfully and after winning the Grand Prix came second in the SA National Championships. He then won the Grand Prix at the Pretoria Show and followed this by winning the 1987 FEI World Cup, the first World Cup I had ever won. It was a very big moment in my life: a World Cup is something every South African aims to win and I doubt I'll ever forget it.

It seemed that Flaunt's run of bad luck was well and truly over, especially as he then went on to be runner-up in the Derby, which was won that year by Gail Foxcroft riding Bye and Bye. Gail won with eight faults and I had 9¼, so had I not had the time faults there would have been a jump-off.

Then, at the very next show, the SA Grand Prix, bad luck hit us again: Flaunt had jumped in the first class but then fell so ill I had to withdraw him from the show. It turned out he'd eaten a cowfeed by mistake, which had temporarily affected his heart muscles. We were back to square one; he had to be rested for another three months.

Despite that, he won the Show-jumper of the Year Award for the most successful horse in the major competitions of 1987.

As one of his fetlocks was slightly windgally, I decided that during this lay-off we would blister him. Of course, with our luck as it was, the blister went terribly wrong and he was left badly scarred. Then (and I firmly believe this was caused by the blister) he threw a fairly large splint at rest on the outside of the near fore which was to cause him quite a lot of pain. Although he wasn't lame when he came back into work, I found that he wasn't happy landing to the right. He would rather land on the wrong leg and do a very quick flying change than land on the leg with the splint — which was fair enough, but as a result, he wasn't his usual self at the Cape Protea Show. Nevertheless, he managed two thirds, one of which was a third to Watchfire in the Grand Prix.

On my return to Johannesburg he was operated on and the splint removed. Flaunt was then left out of work until the beginning of August. I promised myself that I would *not* try and get him ready for the Derby, but I broke that promise and started to get him fit. Then, just three weeks before the Derby, Flaunt went unsound with me while I was cantering him around the sand track at Kyalami Park. This time the offending leg was the off fore and the injury diagnosed as high suspensory. He was out of work for another four months but came back to have a very good win in the accumulator at the 1989 Cape Protea Show. (He beat Watchfire into second place.)

Then, only a couple of weeks later, I competed with him at the Rand Show and just when he looked like winning a major class with a fantastic time in the jump-off, he slipped behind as he took off for the last jump and never got his back legs off the ground. This caused severe lameness behind and put him out of the Royal Show in Pietermaritzburg and Tongaat.

I am glad to say that Flaunt came back to work and ended off 1989 by beating Watchfire into second place at the Pretoria Grand Prix and giving me my eighth win in the South African Show Jumping Championship.

In 1990 Flaunt missed the first big show, the Cape Protea, but was ready to jump at the Rand Show. However in the first round of the Welcome Stakes Watchfire threw me face-first into the top pole of a jump smashing my right cheek bone. I had to have reconstructive and plastic surgery that night so Flaunt didn't get to jump. I was out of action for several weeks but jumped Flaunt at the Royal Show in Pietermaritzburg in May although I had only been back in the saddle for three days. He was runner-up in the Grand Prix and the Accumulator but, a cough and then another injury, meant that the next time he jumped was November. He was runner-up in the Transvaal Championship and won the South African Championship for the second consecutive year while Watchfire was again runner-up. I now have nine South African Championships to my name.

During 1988 I concentrated a great deal on Watchfire, who was purchased off the track as a four-year-old in 1984. He was origi-

Flaunt goes down the bank at the Derby

Overleaf: *Watchfire negotiating a quick turn*

nally bought by Martin Gilbert who told me within a couple of months of having purchased Watchfire that he was a great horse.

Martin had been a pupil of mine for several years and I asked him for an option before I even set eyes on the horse. I followed Watchfire's progress right from the beginning.

As I mentioned when talking about Honey Girl, Watchfire and Honey Girl share the same grandsire and great-grandsire, and Watchfire's sire, Permont, is a full brother to Anneli Wucherpfennig's Seville, so naturally, I was all the more interested in Watchfire since his breeding indicated that he might well be a jumper.

Martin coasted along quietly with Watchfire and I watched him go through D Grade and into C. Then, at the beginning of Watchfire's C Grade career, Martin was approached at a training show by a friend of top A Grade showjumper Ronnie Lawrence with an offer of R20 000 for Watchfire, but Martin turned him down. He didn't really want to sell; anyway, he'd promised first option to me.

Ten minutes later, the agent returned with an increased offer of R25 000 which Martin also turned down, and a third offer of R30 000, also declined.

Every time the bid was raised, Martin came to me to tell me about it and to tell me that there was no way he would sell Watchfire to the interested party, but even so, I began to get a little worried that with this sort of interest shown in Watchfire I might be totally outbid on the horse eventually. I knew Watchfire's potential and I knew that in my hands he would go right to the top. He was, however, also very sensitive which is why Martin was so concerned that I have him.

All this happened a month before the Rand Show, and it was during the Rand Show that I approached Wolfgang Wodrich (who was then my sponsor) and Gail Rosegold with a proposition. Then the three of us made an offer on Watchfire.

Martin really didn't want to sell, but the money (and a very nice horse off the track which he still has today) was almost as good as that previously offered; so a deal was struck and Watchfire was jointly owned by Gail, Wolfgang and myself until the partnership was dissolved and I bought him outright.

The purchase was made at the end of April 1986, so Watchfire jumped through the rest of 1986 as a C Grade with me. I was at this time putting a lot of schooling and work into him so I really went very carefully with him in C Grade and didn't speed him around too much, preferring to bide my time. He is quite a highly strung horse although he doesn't look it. He can't and won't take pressure, so I have had to be careful in training him. Perhaps this is why he copes well with the pressure of competition.

On the subject of pressure, I know that I can be very demanding, but I have always been willing to accept that there are horses who simply can't take pressure and there's no point in trying to force them. Some years ago I had an awkward horse; he was ewe-necked and found it difficult to come down on the bit. I initially took the attitude that he was damn well going to listen to my leg and going to come down on the bit whether he liked it or not, and within days, he was a complete nervous wreck. He simply couldn't take the pressure of being handled in an extremely firm manner; and I don't mean I beat him up — far from it. In the end, I had to alter my entire view of how to handle him and when I softened my approach, he responded. I sold him to an international rider having warned the rider not to pressurise the horse. Fortunately, the rider didn't put pressure on him and both did well.

Watchfire would have been extremely difficult if I had turned the pressure on too soon. However, after he had been in B Grade for about six months, I began to find it difficult to hold him back. I didn't want him to upgrade to A just yet, so I used to go into jump-offs and accumulate something like 10 or 15 time faults so as to be sure of not getting a place. Obviously, every now and again I would put my finger on the pulse and Watchfire would go in and come out with a spectacular win. He was eventually to turn A Grade sometime around August 1987.

As soon as he went into medium A Grade he started to win and he accumulated a lot of points during his first four or five months. He had only jumped in about six A Grade shows before the Cape Protea Show in March 1988 when he was to give me perhaps the most successful year of my showjumping career.

He went first to compete in the medium classes at the Cape Protea Show, and he won the Medium Welcome Stakes with a fantastic jump-off against the clock.

Watchfire displays his brilliance

Flaunt was there as my top horse, but when I realised his splint was worrying him, I decided to put Watchfire into the international class the following day.

I did this after a great deal of thought, and I did no more than nurse Watchfire around quietly. He got a low ticket, I think it was a sixth or a seventh, but it was invaluable experience for him.

The next day I didn't jump him because I had decided to jump him in the Grand Prix the day after. I just wanted to take him in and give him a couple of quiet rounds — again, for the experience.

At the time, I was riding for a new sponsor, Polygon Systems, who had only signed me up about two weeks before I went to the Cape Protea Show, so I really felt obliged to be as competitive as possible in the Grand Prix, especially as it was to be televised.

I jumped Flaunt in the Grand Prix but I didn't push him because of his leg. Consequently, he had a double clear but his time wasn't terribly fast, of course, whereas Anneli had a very fast round with Storm Finch (only to have a jump down) and Barry Taylor was in the lead with a super round on his wonderful horse, Power Force.

I was last to jump and I was very much in two minds about what I ought to do. Should I nurse Watchfire quietly round, it being his first ever Grand Prix? Or should I have a go and try to win?

The course lent itself to Watchfire having a go, for although the course was big and testing, there was nowhere that I had to do a desperate left or right-hand turn into something that might have given him a fright.

As the bell rang, I had one last look around the track and I decided to go for it. Fortunately for me, he flew it, and I brought him out the winner of the Protea Grand Prix.

Two weeks later at the Rand

Show, Watchfire was to be second in the first medium class, after which he developed a virus and did not jump again. Flaunt was out of the show because of his splint, and I had to sit on the grandstand and watch rather than compete. Fortunately, several of my pupils were competing and this helped to make up for not competing myself, especially as one or two of them did exceptionally well.

In 1988 the SA Championship was held at the Royal Show in Pietermaritzburg. I decided to ride Watchfire in all the international classes. I really took it easy with him and put no pressure on him whatsoever. In the accumulator, I only jumped one round as I felt that the second round was far too big for such a young inexperienced A Grade, but he held his own and came third in the Grand Prix and in the SA National Championship.

Several days later I took Watchfire to the Tongaat International Show where I nursed him through the earlier classes and he won the Grand Prix, beating Barry Taylor and Power Force into second place.

After giving him a couple of weeks' rest, I then took him to the Lowveld Show in Nelspruit where the A Grade competitions are not divided into big and small classes, but are open.

As a rule, none of the top A Grades go to the show to compete, so I felt it would do Watchfire a lot of good to have the relaxation of competing in the smaller A Grade competitions for fun. He jumped very well for me and won the Lowveld Championship.

Several weeks later, I took him to the Sun City Indoor International Horse Show. Watchfire had never jumped big classes indoors before and I was quite dubious about how he would go, but once again he really held his own; he won the Grand Prix in fine style (Flaunt's full sister, Fair Flight, took second place), and he came second in the Have a Gamble Stakes, which gave him the Victor Ludorum for the show.

Straight after the Sun City Indoor Show, he was to win me my second FEI World Championship; the following day he swept the boards and won the Transvaal Championship.

We were now nearing the end of the season, and the next major competition coming up was the Dunhill Derby.

Despite Watchfire's previous successes, I felt that the Derby track was too testing for him at this stage; I doubted he was ready for all the banks, dykes, table jumps and funnies that make up a Derby course.

He had jumped a close second to Tony Lewis the previous year in the mini-Derby and I must admit it was tempting to have a go at the real thing, particularly as he had been the fifth highest qualifier for the Derby itself, but I had made up my mind and this was the decision I was going to stick with, so the 1988 Derby saw me sitting on the grandstand.

The day after the competition ended, I took Watchfire to jump over the Derby course. I had lowered the fences to about 1,3 m and I realised then the wisdom of my decision not to jump him in the actual competition, for he was decidedly nervous of some of the funnies and it took at least ten minutes to coax him, with a lead from another horse, down the bank. I attribute all the success I have had over the years to this sort of forethought and careful planning, and I can't recommend strongly enough that the rider who wants to succeed adopt the same policy. It does the horse no end of good. The following year Watchfire had an excellent round at the Derby with only four faults to be second.

The last show of the season, the South African Grand Prix, was held in Welkom ten days after the Derby. Watchfire came out the ultimate victor again, winning the South African Grand Prix and the Showjumper of the Year Award for the most successful horse of 1988.

After a well-deserved rest during November and December, Watchfire came back into light work to get fit and ready for the Cape Protea at the beginning of March.

This was to be the first show where Watchfire would not win since his A Grade career began, although he and I (as Captain) were members of the victorious Springbok team. A couple of weeks after this show, Watchfire came back on form and he won three of the five competitions at the Rand Show: the Accumulator, the Grand Prix, the Championship and the Victor Ludorum.

At the Royal Show in Pietermaritzburg I think he gave himself a fright in the Accumulator when he jumped the wall at 6'1", after that he had mild duck outs at several fences. In August Watchfire was runner-up in the Port Elizabeth Grand Prix while Flaunt took third place. At Sun City Watchfire won both the Welcome and Have a Gamble Stakes but only managed fifth place in the Grand Prix, he once again won the Victor Ludorum. In the Pretoria Grand Prix he was runner-up to Flaunt, in the Derby he was second and in the South African Championship he was once again runner-up to Flaunt. In the end it was a good year and Watchfire won the Lachlan and Bye and Bye Trophy for the most Grand Prix successes. Ronnie Lawrence and High Hopes won the Show Jumper of the Year award.

In 1990 at Watchfire's first show, the Cape Protea, in the run off of the Grand Prix I misjudged a short turn into the last jump and we hit it very hard. Being such a sensitive horse I think this upset him again because at the next show, the Rand Show, I had the accident mentioned earlier. I then did the unheard of and put another rider, Domminy Alexander, on Watchfire the next day to compete in the small classes. I felt that it was imperative to get him back into the ring. Domminy also jumped him at the Royal Show and then he and I won the Grand Prix at the Tongaat Show a few days later. At the next show in Port Elizabeth turning into the last jump Watchfire threw me into the wall grazing my cheek and tearing the earring out of my ear which required six stitches. We still managed to win the Grand Prix the following day.

At Sun City Watchfire won the Grand Prix and in the FEI World Championship was 0,58 seconds behind Peter Gotz in a very exciting finish. He was runner-up again in the Derby and the South African Championship. Last but not least Watchfire and I were once again given the Showjumper of the Year award.

As I write, I can see Honey Girl, Watchfire, Flaunt, All the Aces, several B and C Grade horses and a promising four-year-old which was raced until only a few months ago. It's like looking at my past and my future all together, and it strikes me that I'm far from finished yet. With luck, I'll compete in top competitions for at least another eight years and I hope that in that time, South African riders will be allowed to compete internationally. It is a tragedy that some of the exceptional horses and riders we have in this country cannot compete overseas. There is no doubt in my mind that if they are allowed to do so, they will *more* than hold their own with the best, and I'm looking forward to them being given the opportunity to prove it.

Watchfire

Overleaf: *Watchfire after winning the 1988 FEI Championship*

10

Training Showjumpers

A GREAT deal has been written about how to train showjumpers and most of the good books say the same thing. For that reason, I have tried to avoid repeating what can be found in those books. I have concentrated instead on how to train the ex-racehorse because, by comparison, little has been written about it.

This chapter is aimed at people who already have a working knowledge of how to ride a horse; people who are serious enough about their sport to have equipped themselves with a competent trainer. I hope you will bear in mind that although this chapter appears to cover the complete training of the horse from novice to advanced, it is only a skeleton, a solid foundation that you can only hope to pad out with experience.

I have been able to outline certain exercises, tell you their purpose and explain what the entire picture should look like, but it wasn't possible for me to incorporate experience, talent, nerve, learning ability, competitive instinct or feel into these pages. Nor was it possible for me to incorporate "everything there is to know about training a horse", partly because I don't profess to know everything myself, and partly because the variables are infinite. The entire content of this book could have been devoted to the training of the novice horse in his first year under saddle, and still I would have left a great deal unsaid.

That realisation left me wondering whether I should write anything on the subject of training at all; for it wasn't so much a case of, Where do I begin? as, Where do I end?

In short, to try to crush a lifetime's experience between the covers of a book has not been easy, but I believe I have managed to set out a thorough working guide and I hope it will be of practical assistance to all who use it.

CHOOSING A POTENTIAL SHOWJUMPER

The majority of horses available to South African riders come straight off the track.

Fortunately, we have the finest possible type of thoroughbred in this country: he is a big, substantial, sensible horse, and often he makes an excellent showjumper.

Almost all the horses I have ever owned came off the track, and over the years I've developed a fairly successful knack of picking out which ones are most likely to jump.

I have outlined below the things I look for in a horse, my main requirements being that he is sound and that he has a good temperament.

Soundness speaks for itself. Nobody in his right mind is going to buy an unsound horse, and you shouldn't leave anything to chance: always have a horse vetted and, providing the price warrants it, include X-rays of his feet as well as his legs in the vetting.

Soundness and temperament are of equal importance to me because a horse with a suitable temperament is no good if he's unsound, and a sound horse is equally useless if he lacks a good temperament.

However, when I talk about a horse having a good temperament, I don't just mean that he must be sensible to handle; some horses are quite easy to handle, but they are perhaps obstinate, lazy, unintelligent or ungenuine in some way, which renders them as useless as a neurotic horse.

Ideally, the horse should also have a bold outlook because this is no job for a chicken. At the same time, he mustn't be so brave he's a danger to everyone within a 5 km radius; he must have an instinct for self-preservation.

With regard to size, I can only advise you not to overhorse yourself. Make sure you feel really comfortable with the size of horse you choose because it can make all the difference to whether you and he are going to click and make a winning team.

I'm a fairly tall person at 1,73 m, and yet I rarely ever consider a horse over 16h.2ins because I feel far more comfortable on a horse of 16h or 16h.1in. However, I feel uncomfortable on anything smaller than 15h.3ins, and I wouldn't buy such a horse for myself even though many horses under 15h.3ins are perfectly capable of carrying a person of my height round an adult A Grade course.

Figure 10.1

Figure 10.2

I am fairly flexible when it comes to considering a horse's age — probably more so than most people. Occasionally I buy a three-year-old, but I prefer older horses because three-year-olds have to be turned away and my facilities are not geared towards having numerous young horses dotted around the property.

I will happily take a seven-year-old because I don't consider him too old to teach; it would be a bit late in the day for a potential dressage horse, but a potential showjumper soon learns his job.

If everything about him is right, I will even take an eight or nine-year-old, particularly if I like his breeding, there being no doubt in my mind that some bloodlines produce jumpers.

I believe that a horse can jump international A Grade successfully, that is to say, win consistently in this country, for five to eight years if he is looked after properly; but no matter how well a horse appears or seems to be going, I don't like jumping a horse older than 17. To do so is like asking a 60-year-old athlete to continue competing at top level.

On the subject of balance, I like a horse that can carry himself, a horse that does not have a natural tendency to go on the forehand. I bear in mind that the majority of racehorses go on the forehand because they haven't been trained to lighten up in front, but the horse's general conformation will tell you whether he is likely to find it easy to learn to let his haunches do the work for a change.

Obviously, I look for good conformation. I know that in the majority of books conformation is put at the top of the list, but the truth is, I will buy a ewe-necked, cow-hocked, calf-kneed monstrosity if he's a proven top winner and an A Grade that hasn't shown a day's unsoundness. Naturally, I prefer a horse to have good conformation, but as with soundness and temperament, it's no good on its own.

That said, there is no doubt that the better a horse's conformation, the more likely it is that he will remain sound throughout his career. It is also true that the nearer the horse is to the ideal conformation the easier he is to school, since he finds the work easier to execute. He is also more comfortable to ride, but that's merely a bonus.

There was a time in the 1960s and 1970s when I preferred a horse to be straight through the hock because I believed such horses were better jumpers. I no longer hold that view because experience has taught me that jumpers come with a variety of hocks: I have seen even sickle and cow-hocked horses jumping A Grade courses. One of my top A Grades, Flaunt, has the worst cow hocks imaginable. If I'd turned him down because of his hocks, I'd have missed one of the best horses I've ever had. However, I have to admit that I much prefer my horse to have a good length from point of hip to hock, and then a straight line to the ground. This gives the appearance of the hock being close to the ground.

I also like a horse to have a good top line, because such horses tend to work through easily and carry themselves well.

A horse with a good shoulder also tends to have good self-carriage and is better able to move freely in front than other horses. When I say that I like a horse to move freely, I don't mean that I look for an exaggerated and showy action; the action must simply be free, that's all.

I won't take an unproven horse that is back at the knee or tied in below the knee because the chances of his legs giving trouble are higher than I would like. I also steer clear of splay-footed horses because they too tend to go unsound.

Speaking of knees, I do like a horse to have a high knee action because in my experience such horses tend to jump well.

I wouldn't turn down a horse that dishes, because dishing has never affected a horse's performance. It is something to avoid in the show or dressage horse, but it hardly matters in the showjumper. Honey Girl dished but it didn't stop her from winning every major competition of her day. Having said that, I should imagine dishing puts extra strain on the joints, although I have never known of an unsoundness occurring through it.

Plenty of hunting people will tell you that a pigeon-toed horse is a danger to ride. I've had quite a few and I'm still here, but perhaps that's because I choose horses with a high knee action.

I don't mind a horse being a little long in the back, but the back mustn't be too long — 10 cm at the most — because a long back is often a weak back; also, long-backed horses find it difficult to collect and/or work through.

I am averse to most vices, but I particularly dislike a horse that rears. I don't care how good he is — if he rears, he is dangerous and therefore useless as far as I'm concerned.

On the subject of vices, I should mention that I will buy a windsucker. Contrary to what is said about this vice, I have never found it to cause a horse to lose condition. Perhaps I just feed my horses well and windsucking doesn't knock the condition off as it would on a less "well done" horse, but I don't think that's the case. I believe windsucking causes me more stress than the horse because it happens to drive me round the bend.

I pay a lot of attention to breeding because courage, jumping ability and temperament are frequently traits in certain bloodlines, just as they are lacking in others. There is the occasional freak whose parentage would lead one to believe he can't possibly have so much as a hop in him but who will astound you by making a Grand Prix horse, but such horses are rare. With thoroughbreds, one usually knows more or less what one has if one looks into the pedigree, but it would be a big mistake to allow unfavourable breeding to persuade you to turn down a horse that appears to have every other quality necessary in a top class showjumper.

When I go to a trainer's yard to try a horse, I like him to be able to canter on both legs within the first two times of my asking him to do so, even if he canters a little fast. If he can't do it, he's probably stiff on one rein, having favoured that one leg in gallop all the time. Notwithstanding all that, a horse that is basically well balanced will soon click on to what is being asked of him and will canter on both reins.

When trying out a horse that is still in training, I do jump him, but only over straw bales, which are quite substantial looking by comparison with a pole. I feel that a pole does not invite a horse that has possibly never jumped in his life to pick up his legs and clear it. Also, a horse is less likely to give his legs a knock if he fails to jump a straw bale, and you must consider the trainer; it's not fair on him if the horse knocks his legs up and you then decide you don't want him.

Sometimes I see a "going horse" I take a liking to, one I have perhaps seen competing, and if that happens, the first thing I do is secure a first option in the event that the owner should decide to sell him. I then watch his progress and ability in the ring and if and when he comes up for sale, I ask the owner to let me try him, preferably on my home ground.

I'm not inclined to buy a horse after the first time I've ridden him, so if I still like him, I then ask the owner to let me try him a few times more, but I don't believe in overjumping somebody else's horse to perhaps test how high he can jump. The few times that I ride him at home are spent working him mostly on the flat and over reasonable fences to see whether he is happy to adapt to the way I would ultimately want him to go for me.

Taking for granted that I am now impressed, and providing the price is within my reach, I then agree to purchase the horse subject to a thorough examination by my vet, which also means that several X-rays must be included in the vetting.

After purchase, it could take anything from a month to four months before I produce this horse in the ring, depending on how quickly he adapts to my way of asking him to go, particularly as I like my horses to be very obedient. I don't enjoy a horse that rushes his fences, drops the bit a stride or two out or hesitates on takeoff, and any such problems must be sorted out before I will consider taking a new horse to a show.

I like a horse to feel good in the air and to use himself reasonably well, but he doesn't have to over-bascule. He must be neat in front, and (this is important to me) he must use his back behind the saddle, over the fence.

I don't like a horse that pulls his hind legs up underneath him over his jump, although, obviously, every horse must draw his hind legs up to a certain extent. However, it is the up and outward hind-leg action that I prefer.

Two of the faults I most frequently find when trying horses that have already been graded are (a) the horse doesn't approach his fence in a straight line but swings his hindquarters to the inside or outside (often, this type of horse does the same thing on landing) and (b) the horse doesn't know how to lead with the correct leg upon landing. It amazes me how little effort is put into teaching a horse to do this in the early stages of his jumping career.

However, I realised long ago that the perfect horse is impossible to find, and I will put up with a lot from a horse that can jump and has the right temperament for the job. The only thing I *won't* chance is an unsafe horse (whether through temperament or physical fault).

The criteria upon which I choose my horses are the same ones I would apply to non-thoroughbreds if it so happened that I preferred them. Why do I like thoroughbreds so much? Because they are quick thinking, quick learning, and true athletes. If one can find a thoroughbred with the right temperament, he is, quite simply, very hard to beat.

TRAINING THE EX-RACEHORSE

Training guides normally begin by discussing how to back and school a horse that may be halter broken and handled, but is otherwise totally green.

I haven't started this training section like that because, as I have said before, I have rarely bought a horse that didn't come from a racing stable. Of all the horses I've had since I was in juniors, only Gunga Din and Formaat were non-thoroughbred and consequently, retraining ex-racehorses has become my speciality. Also, there are so many books dealing with the subject of breaking and training the untouched youngster that I

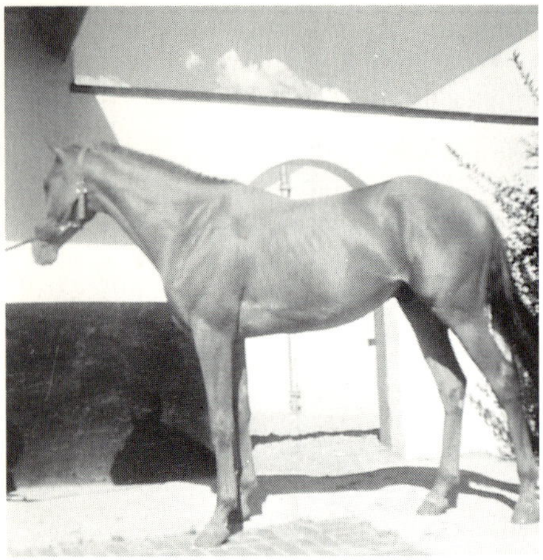
Flaunt just off the track, aged three

Flaunt as a six year old

can't see any point in repeating it all here. So few books concentrate on coping with ex-racehorses that I hope what I have to say will be of some interest and use, particularly as the majority of South African riders are in the same position as I am: they buy ex-racehorses in the hope that they will jump.

We all know that few ex-racehorses ever shake off their early training so completely that it is not possible to tell they were once trained for racing, and we also know that the ex-racehorse is going to be more difficult to school as a result of the habits he has picked up while in training. Nevertheless, we're going to try to rehabilitate the ex-racehorse, if only because most of us have no choice.

So, after purchasing your horse and bringing him home:

- Have his teeth checked and rasped if necessary.
- Change his shoes from racing plates to ordinary shoes.
- De-worm him.
- Decide whether to turn the horse away for three months, and base your decision on:
  — his condition
  — his mental state.

If the horse has had a hard racing career, he may be tucked up after coming off the track. You can't do anything constructive with him until he's been given a chance to relax and let down, so feed him an appropriate diet until he ceases to have that tucked-up appearance.

If you decide to turn the horse away to let down, he should be out in the paddock in the day and stabled at night. Make sure he has adequate outside shelter from heat and hard weather.

I never put two horses out together because when I was seven, my father's horse kicked out playfully at a pony of mine, breaking her leg. That taught me a valuable lesson and all my paddocks are double fenced with a 2,7 m gap between them. I don't allow my horses any contact whatsoever, and the walls dividing my stables are 3 m high so that the horses cannot even touch noses. I have done this because experience has taught me that thoroughbreds tend to kick out in the paddock or at the stable walls when excited and many injuries can occur as a result.

For the horse at grass, it is a good idea to turn him out from ten in the morning until three in the afternoon and make sure he has plenty of water. If you live in a part of the country that is particularly hot in summer, do the horse a favour and bring him into a stable during the hottest part of the day rather than leaving him outside to cook.

If you decide to turn the horse away, first hack him around the field — just to see what he feels like. I always trot a new horse over a pole on the ground several times and then put a cross pole up from ankle height to 45 cm to see whether he pings, flops, stops, runs out, naps, puts his ears back or runs away upon landing. I do this purely to get an idea of what his attitude to life is.

Don't fiddle with him (and by that, I mean don't try loose schooling him over jumps or hauling him around the plot). You've taken the decision of turning him away, so stick to it and leave him alone to relax.

BRINGING THE RESTED HORSE INTO WORK

Before you bring the rested horse into work, consider the following:

- *Food.* As a general rule, it's wise to keep the horse on a maintenance ration at this stage. He isn't going to do anything strenuous for a few months, and unless he starts losing condition, basic cubes and hay will be all he needs.
- *Tack.* Make sure that the tack you choose for your horse fits well and is suitable for the job. The following items are constantly in use in my yard:
  - — I usually get my horses going in a thick hollow-mouthed Stubben egbutt. A fidgety horse usually goes best in this type of bit.
  - — My second choice is a medium-sized hollow-mouthed loose ring snaffle. I don't like rubber snaffles because they don't give a true feeling.
  - — Horses that are strong in the mouth might go well in a twisted snaffle or perhaps a Waterford, which is the stronger of these two. This bit should only be used by a knowledgeable person and perhaps on the advice of an instructor. It isn't as severe as a double wire snaffle which should definitely only be used in expert hands.
  - — I find a flash noseband suits most horses. Some strong horses go well if the cavesson is fairly tight; other strong horses relax if the cavesson is kindly adjusted. The drop part must not be tight; it must simply be comfortable for the horse. Experiment with it — find out how your horse goes best in it.
  - — I always carry either a crop or a schooling whip, the latter for the flat work.
  - — I usually ride my horses in light plastic spurs with the actual spur filed down blunt to half a centimetre in length. Racehorses often have no idea what the leg means. They must learn to go forward from the leg, but often a strong leg can upset a horse until he learns what it's all about. It might seem a little strange that some racehorses don't go forward, but unfortunately, it's all too true. There is a big difference between a horse going forward from the leg and a horse going in a flat-out gallop. If a horse is very hot I don't ride him in spurs at all, but I use my leg strongly whenever necessary.
  - — I am now going to say something I don't want you to misconstrue: when I get a horse off the track, I put him in draw reins. This is because 90% of the horses I buy have a high head carriage. In their unrelaxed state, such horses can sometimes be a little peacocky or even hollow and it can be difficult to encourage them down onto the bit. Some horses no longer need draw reins after a couple of weeks — others after six months. Then again, there are horses who benefit from draw reins throughout their entire career, even if they are only used now and again to remind the horse of the correct frame and perhaps to encourage

Flaunt working in draw reins

him into a longer, lower outline. However, bear in mind that there is no quicker route to ruining a good horse than the incorrect use of draw reins, and I am reluctant to mention that I use them at all in case the less experienced rider misunderstands what I am saying. In fact, I believe that only a top rider — and I do not mean someone who has been riding for 20 years, I mean a rider of international standard — should use draw reins without supervision, because irreversible harm can be done to a horse's balance and carriage if draw reins are badly employed. A rider uses draw reins correctly by riding the horse on the snaffle rein, *not* on the draw rein. The draw rein should only be used to encourage the horse to keep a longer, lower head carriage. His chin should be in line with that part of the underside of the neck that comes out of the chest. At no time must the horse be hauled in.

— I put a running martingale on all my horses: it makes for greater control. But a running martingale should only come into play as a form of correction; it shouldn't come into play at all if the horse is going on the bit correctly.

THE FIRST THREE MONTHS

Begin by hacking the horse around the countryside for six weeks, regardless of whether he has been turned away or brought straight into work after purchase. Use dirt roads you know to be quiet and fairly free of traffic, preferably in the company of a more sensible horse. You will have greater control if you put draw reins on the horse at this stage, but remember what I said about draw reins: they should only come into play if you really need them.

After hacking the horse out for a few weeks, begin to take every opportunity to jump him over small natural obstacles such as fallen logs or, at a later stage, the odd ditch, preferably with a lead from another horse. Don't put him to anything trappy or anything he is likely to be unsure about; just make his jumping easy and happy from the very beginning.

After about six weeks of this sort of lifestyle, start working him in the school.

I would like to mention here that when you ride (and particularly when you jump) horses, you must stay alert and ahead of everything the horse might do. When driving a car, you keep your eyes open for situations that might cause a problem, and when riding a horse you should be doing the same thing.

- Begin by walking 30 m circles in the school (still in draw reins) and ask for a light inside bend by drawing lightly on the snaffle rein, sometimes in a backward and sometimes in an outward (flexing) movement. Make sure you use plenty of inside leg; maintain an even contact on the outside rein and put your outside leg slightly behind the girth so that the horse doesn't swing his quarters away from the inside leg which is often the stronger (see photograph at left).
- Walk four or five 30 m circles to the left and four or five to the

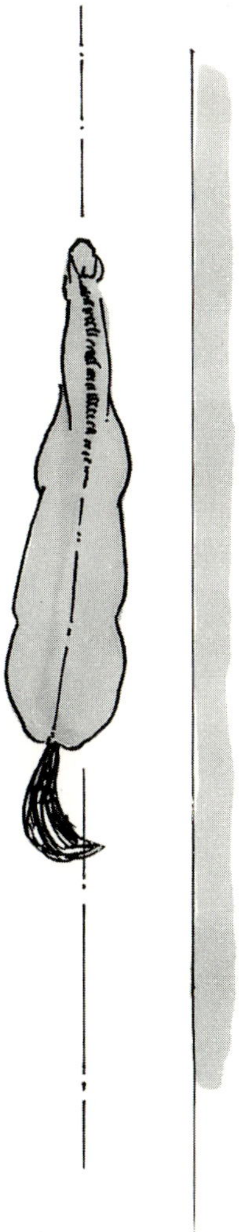

Figure 10.3

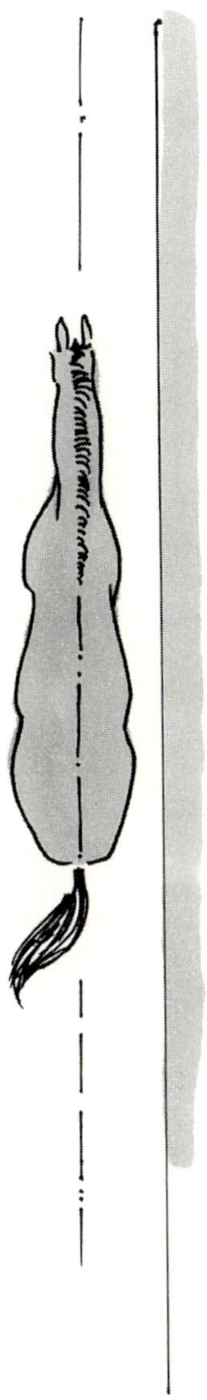

Figure 10.4

right, then ride the horse round the outside of the school. Change the rein and repeat the work. Then repeat the exercise at the trot. Each time you change the rein, remember to change the diagonal also so that the horse becomes even and supple on both reins. The young horse will usually be ready for a break by this time, so give him a loose rein (a horse should have a loose rein for at least three or four minutes) and a pat before repeating the entire exercise.

- After a week or two of this type of work, you can start to ask for 20 m circles. You can also start to do half loops by going up the long side of the school and, at the corner, making a half turn back to the long side so that you end up in the opposite direction.
- When you are riding on the straight, don't allow your horse to let his hindquarters drift to the inside. Any horse will do this if he can because he likes to "cling" to the wall of the school with his shoulder. The trick is to keep the horse's outside shoulder away from the wall by riding "inside leg to outside rein". (A trainer must help you learn how to do this if you are uncertain.) Figure 10.3 shows you the position of the forehand and the quarters when the rider allows his horse's hindquarters to drift into the inside. As you can see, the horse isn't straight. The hindquarters are slightly wider than the forehand so if the horse is allowed to cling to the wall, the hindquarters have nowhere else to go, but in. Figure 10.4 shows the correction.
- As the horse progresses, your half turns back to the track can become smaller so that they are 15 m and (very much later) 10 m in diameter.

Do all the above exercises at the walk and in rising trot and don't canter the horse at all during this stage. All you need to ask of him is that he goes forward and that he maintains a good rhythm. Bear in mind that a horse at this stage of his training will find even this comparatively simple task quite difficult to do.

- When riding these exercises, be careful not to over-turn your horse's head to the inside. I would rather see a horse riding a circle without any bend in his neck whatsoever than see him with the neck over-bulged to the outside. This neck bulge to the outside results from too much inside rein. When a horse is correctly bent to the inside, you should only see the outline of the inside eye. Anything more is excessive. Colonel Dudgeon gave me this hint many years ago: see that your horse's ear tips are always level. When the outside ear tip is lower, you know that the horse is tilting his head and stiffening his neck. If this happens, use more inside leg to put him onto the outside rein. Tilting is a habit that once established, is hard to eradicate. It can stem from two things: one is the perpetual use of too much inside rein, and the other is asking the horse to perform exercises of which he is not capable. Horses that are asked to cope with two track before they are supple enough to do so often use tilting as an evasion.
- As I have said before, at this stage you need not ask for anything more than that the horse goes forward in a rhythmical trot. After he has become established in this work

Pharaoh's Diadem in correct canter

(which may take two weeks, or it may take two months), you can ask him to canter. The same principles apply: ask only for a forward-going and even canter, for to ask for any degree of collection in any of the paces at this stage would be detrimental to the horse's balance, outline and attitude to going forward. If you feel the canter pace is a little fast, don't worry about it, providing the horse is going forward from the leg into your hand. It is far better at this stage to let the horse *go on* than to try to check him and perhaps disturb his balance. What you *don't* want at this stage is a horse that appears to be cantering in collection, for in the novice horse, such a feeling can only stem from the fact that the horse isn't going forward; he is merely bouncing around. It may *feel* like a collected canter, but it is unlikely that the horse is working through from behind — this is what I call cantering backwards. *Don't allow it.* Push him on. (See photograph at left.)

- On the plus side, the "rocking horse" type, the type who canters backwards given half a chance, usually develops a good collected canter more easily and quickly than his counterpart when the time is right to ask him for it, *providing* you can get it through forward movement.
- You can only start to slow the canter work down when the horse is completely balanced and is moving unhesitatingly away from the leg and maintaining an even rhythm at all paces.
- Remember that it is easy to bore or sour your horse. To avoid this, hack him at least two out of six working days a week, but while hacking, put into practice everything the horse is learning during his lessons.

Horses, especially young horses, find all this work mentally and muscularly difficult, and although it is not feasible for most of us to follow the regimen of the old horse masters who would work a horse for 15 minutes twice a day, it is worth bearing in mind that their methods were effective because they had grasped that the young horse finds it difficult to concentrate for longer than 15 minutes per schooling session.

Finally, after the horse has been worked, he should be walked cool, watered and then turned out into the paddock for a good roll and a pick at the grass to help him relax.

THE NEXT THREE MONTHS

It's time to start asking more of your horse. By now he should be moving forward from the leg and he should be working on the bit, preferably without the help of draw reins.

- Start making the circles smaller and beware of the horse ceasing to go forward at this stage. A horse finds it much easier to trot small circles if he is allowed to drag himself slowly around on his front legs: if he tries this, give him a good half halt and drive him through from behind.
- Start sitting into your horse by asking for a few strides in

sitting trot and rise again if he stiffens or hollows his back. Increase the number of strides until your horse can carry you without hollowing or stiffening, and build up the amount of time you ask for sitting trot until your horse can carry you comfortably. Once again, keep him going forward. This is easier said than done. It can take weeks; in some cases (especially if a horse's conformation makes it difficult for him to round his back and neck) you can struggle with a horse for months before he will round his back and carry you while you sit into him. But you can't expect any horse to carry you comfortably if you're not supple enough to sit into him without stiffening yourself. When a rider bounces around on a horse's back, the horse finds it just as uncomfortable as the rider. The only answer is to get a good trainer to lunge you until you have established a good seat and can sit into your horse without hampering him.

- Repeat at the sitting trot the work the horse has done to date.

Maybe I should add here that I ride without stirrups quite often because it keeps me deep in the saddle and helps me to retain a very correct seat. It also prevents me from stiffening up, which is particularly important to me as I suffered an injury while race riding in 1965 and I've had a back problem ever since. Apparently, I pulled the ligaments supporting two vertebrae, L4 and L5, and because I didn't see a doctor for two years following the accident, the ligaments didn't knit properly. As a result, I've been forced to wear a back brace since 1973 and although I don't wear it during competitions, I always wear it at home.

Plenty of riders will tell you that riding without stirrups aggravates a back problem, but I believe that's because most people don't sit properly. They stiffen against the horse, whereas a deep and supple seat should prevent any jarring of the spine. I'm convinced that riding without stirrups helps keep me supple enough to prevent my back problem from getting worse. Having said that, I accept that some back injuries, especially those that cause the vertebrae to fuse, cannot be helped by any amount of sitting, and that after such an injury, any form of riding is bad for the back. It has to be left to the rider's common sense (all too often eclipsed by the desire to ride) to consider then whether to give up the sport, keep it as a hobby or stop riding altogether — a daunting thought.

- When the horse is capable of three and four loop serpentines at the sitting trot while maintaining the rhythm and changing the bend without any resistance, you can start to teach him some two track.
- Start by teaching the horse to leg yield. The purpose of this exercise is to teach the horse to move forward and away from the leg. The leg yield can be executed firstly at the walk and then at the trot, since it isn't a particularly strenuous exercise and the novice horse can manage it without mental or physical stress. I also use a turn on the forehand because, if done correctly, this too will teach a horse to move away from the leg quite effectively.
- When the horse is fluent in leg yield, I teach him shoulder-in. Done correctly, this is one of the most valuable exercises the horse will ever learn. It is a three track exercise, the whole

point being that there is no more than a slight inside bend, and that the horse is tracking up with inside hind to outside fore. I do this exercise on the long side of the school, but at a (much) later stage, I also do it on a circle.

- After mastering shoulder-in, the horse can be taught travers, and the most important thing to remember about riding travers is that the forehand must remain straight on the track while the rider asks the horse to bring his quarters into the school. Horses find this exercise difficult, so don't ask for too much in the early stages; be satisfied if the quarters come in, say, 15 cm at the most, and then increase the bend until the travers is being ridden correctly.
- It may surprise some people that I bother with two track because many believe that two track belongs firmly to the dressage rider and that it offers no real advantage to the showjumper. I can only say that the better a horse's flat work the greater his chance of making A Grade since most horses that can jump well enough are hampered by being poorly schooled. If a horse isn't obedient to the leg; if he can't shorten or lengthen his stride when you ask him to do so; if he isn't balanced and supple, he simply won't be able to negotiate the distances between jumps accurately and with sufficient impulsion to clear them.
- I believe in working a potential showjumper in a paddock full of jumps where he can get used to the sight of them and learn not to worry about them. Make use of them; change the rein around them in large and small figures of eight, bending the horse on both reins around them. This also helps to test whether he is listening to the leg, especially if he is a spooky type of horse.

A young horse off the track

- During the early stages of his training, I am more concerned with getting the horse to listen to my leg and go forward than anything else, but by the time the ex-racehorse has been in work for six to nine months, he should be doing this. He should be working on the bit, preferably without draw reins, and he should be capable of a leg yield and a travers. Remember that some horses might need draw reins for some considerable time, but it's better to work with a view to dispensing with them as quickly as possible.
- During the horse's initial schooling, I start to trot him over trotting poles. As a rule, I begin by using cavaletti, adjusting so that the poles are lying on the ground at a distance of approximately 1,2 m apart, depending on the size of the horse's stride and also on his temperament. I make sure that the horse goes straight over the trotting poles; that he does not deviate left or right and that he maintains an even rhythm. The first few times he does the exercise I allow him to stretch his head and neck down so that he can take a look at the poles, but thereafter, he must be on the bit, between hand and leg, and he must go over the poles *in both directions* as though they were not even there (see photograph top left).
- From the above exercise, I graduate to an ankle height vertical 3 m away from the trotting pole. This is an exercise I never dispense with, and over the months and years the vertical gradually increases in height.

- If a horse has a hot temperament, I usually shorten the distance between the trotting poles to begin with, because a hot horse will sometimes either become very tense during this exercise, or he will trot over one pole and then try to jump out of (or over) the rest. This needs immediate correction: I bring the horse to a halt straight away and I make him stand quietly for half a minute before asking him to repeat the exercise. I don't get irritable and cross with any of the novice horses because to do so only upsets them and makes them worse. Remember, they don't understand what you want and it takes patience to teach them.

- I repeat the exercise until the horse is totally confident. At the same time , I start trotting him over a small cross pole. However, before I start trotting him over any jumps, I take the draw reins off (I may already have dispensed with them, depending on the horse and his needs) because I don't want to restrict the horse's neck. To restrict him would cause him to hollow and stiffen. Worse still, it would damage his balance and self-carriage. I use a cross pole because it guides the horse to the middle of the fence, the sides being higher and therefore more of an effort for him to jump. The cross pole should be roughly 35 cm in the middle and the cups should be placed in the wings so that the sides of the cross pole are not too high. A good jump is 80% approach to 20% actual jump, and I work on perfecting the horse's approach from the start of his training. When he turns into the jump, it must be a good round turn and then he must go straight on to the jump. This is where teaching him to leg yield pays off. After a few days to a week, the cross pole can be raised so that it is 50 cm or 60 cm in the middle.
- From the beginning, I jump my horse towards and away from the stable, and I vary the colour of the poles I use. I don't allow my horses to run off after jumping the cross pole. I insist that they come back to trot as soon as possible. If a horse refuses to listen to me and tries to dash off, I'm not afraid to be tough with him and if I have to I will bring him back to hand by using as hard a half halt as I need to get him to listen and think twice about doing it again. If that doesn't help, I'll often bring the horse right back to halt.
- I then return to using trotting poles and I place three trotting poles in front of a cross pole that has been reduced from 60 cm back to 35 cm. The third trotting pole should be 2,74 m before the cross pole. When the horse is confident, I start to raise the

cross pole so that the horse is trotting over the three trotting poles and then over the cross pole, which is now 60 cm again. Then I start to build a small vertical instead of the cross and I raise its height as the horse progresses.

- At the same time I introduce the horse to a straight pole 40 to 60 cm in height and I put ground poles 30 cm either side of it so that I can jump from either direction.

It has probably taken the horse approximately three weeks to execute the above exercises (from trotting poles to a small vertical) with confidence and accuracy. During this time, as I mentioned before, I have introduced the horse to a 35 cm to 60 cm vertical jump on its own. When he is able to cope with all the above, I introduce him to tiny spreads by doing the following:

- I put up a cross pole 35 cm in height, and 40 to 50 cm behind it, I put a back pole which is 40 to 50 cm high. I use a ground pole but not a takeoff pole; in other words, the pole on the ground is very close to the cross and not pulled out at all. Remember that the horse is still trotting into his jumps so the spread mustn't be too wide for him to cope with it.
- I have been varying the colour and location of the jumps throughout these exercises and now I start to introduce different types of jumps. The horse is going to learn not to worry about:
  - Painted oil drums. Lie them on their side and let him go up and look and touch them with his nose if he wants to (see photograph top left).
  - Wooden boxes, brightly painted, fairly solid looking and between 30 and 50 cm high.
  - Gates, rustic and painted, about 1 m in height and set at a 45° angle to make it smaller to begin with; when the horse is used to jumping a gate set at an angle, you can *gradually* straighten it up until it becomes a vertical.
  - Tyres, brush and anything else you can use as a filler, but remember that with the complete novice, always let him walk up and have a good look before facing him with unusual objects.

The horse must learn to jump spooky obstacles confidently. He is still trotting into the jumps, and I want him to concentrate and to be calm and straight.

- Once the horse is trotting between different vertical and small spread fences up to 80 cm or 90 cm, I feel he can be asked to cope with a double. Put the jump down a couple of holes; approximately 9 m to 10 m away (making two short strides) erect another small upright. Once he's jumping this confidently, go to one stride between two fences with a distance of about 6,5 m between them. This distance should allow the horse level strides between the two jumps, and over a period of weeks, you can build up the height of the jump until it is back at 70 cm. Remember, we are still trotting the jumps. Once we're cantering the jumps, the distance between them must be increased to 7,3 m and 10,7 m depending on whether there should be one or two strides between the jump.
- The horse can now be asked to tackle a course of small jumps,

A young horse trotting into a small fence

and it is not asking too much to expect him to go over a couple of uprights, a spread or two, a row of drums, a small gate, boxes and an upright filled with tyres or brush. I might even ask the horse to cope with a normal related distance of, say, five or six strides. Remember that we are still trotting into our jumps. However, if the horse begins to canter of his own accord, provided I feel his balance at this stage to be good enough, rather than pull him back immediately I let him canter between the fences in a quiet and controlled manner. Then I bring him back to trot. I don't push for a specific number of strides if he canters on after a jump because he's not ready to cope with that just yet. To push him for such a thing at this stage would unbalance him and perhaps drain some of the precious confidence we have built up over the past six months.

Although we are still trotting into our jumps, the horse should now be cantering calmly in his flat work when asked to do so. His upward and downward transitions should be smooth. By now, I am beginning to get an idea of his attitude to the whole showjumping scene. I take him to paddocks belonging to friends so that he can jump over a different set of jumps in strange surroundings, and if his attitude is good, I start taking him to training shows: at least four or five shows before I enter him in the Novice D classes.

Ex-racehorses can be quite excitable at their first couple of shows. This is because they think they're going to race; and it takes them a couple of shows to settle down. I always see to it that my horses are taken to hack around at a few shows before actually going to compete and in this respect I am lucky to have Kyalami Park just next door to me.

I give a lot of voice commands to my horses both when competing and when at home. I don't mean I chat nonsense to them the whole time, but I do give them a good pat, tell them "good boy" in a gentle, slow voice, or if necessary a firm "No", while "Whoa" is also a command my horses are very used to; this teaches them to respond to my voice.

I remember one occasion when Flaunt was a B Grade and I was schooling him in a rubber snaffle. (As I have already mentioned, I don't like rubber snaffles because they don't give a true feel, but for some reason, I had Flaunt in one at that time.)

During the schooling session, the chain in the centre of the rubber snaffle broke and the bit simply fell apart. I was riding him quite strongly into the bridle at the time as I was having trouble with his flying changes, and as the bit broke, I fell back, giving him a fright. The fright, coupled with the sudden loss of the bit from his mouth, caused him to leap into a gallop and in the split second that I was wondering what to do about it, I remembered that whenever Flaunt does something well I lean forward and give him a pat and tell him he's a good boy. He then thinks he's finished and he stops without me pulling him up. This is what I did as he galloped around the school and Flaunt came quickly to a walk. I think we probably avoided a potentially dangerous fall, simply because Flaunt had learned to respond to my voice.

D GRADE

A schooled horse approaching a fence in an active canter

I might take a horse to two training shows before I enter him in the Novice D classes. On the other hand, I might spend six months going to training shows, depending on the horse's attitude and ability. If I have a horse that shows tremendous talent but is a little slow in gaining confidence, I take the time and trouble to take him to however many training shows he needs before he's ready to go into D Grade.

As with the training shows, I use D Grade as a training ground. I might stay there for six months and I don't care if I have to trot all the way around and collect time penalties. I'm not in the least interested in winning and I certainly don't intend jumping against the clock or forcing my horse into anything he's not ready for. This is because I've got my sights firmly set on international A Grade. The hobby rider can collect the prizes in D Grade — the chances are, he's never going to get out of there, whereas, when the time is right, I'll upgrade a far more capable and confident horse (but then, this is my profession and not my hobby).

The one thing I won't stand for at home or at a show is bad behaviour from a horse. I don't appreciate a horse trying to push me over and I won't allow a horse even to rub his head on me after I've worked him and he's being unsaddled. Needless to say, I won't stand for a horse biting, kicking out at the leg aid, napping, ducking around or bucking to unseat me and I correct him immediately if he does any of these things. The odd playful wriggle I will accept, but only for a short while and not too often. I'll also put up with a fun kick-up type of buck when out hacking but I won't stand for it in the school. My one exception is to allow Flaunt to leap a metre or two in the air from time to time because he's not actually trying to buck me off. It's just his way of letting me know that he's enjoying life and he's never playful or disobedient when the pressure is on.

Before we discuss schooling the D Grade over poles, let's take a look at what he should now be capable of on the flat:

- Although far from schooled to an advanced level, he should now be a responsive and pleasant ride.
- The horse also has some show experience and his confidence over poles has improved both at home and in strange surroundings. He is now cantering his courses and it is time to ask a little more of him.

I often use the Pullman exercises, which I find excellent, especially for the D and C Grade horse, but the exercises I favour for the Novice D to D Grade are as follows:

- I trot over trotting poles and pop over a vertical. I always start with this exercise.
- I then trot and canter into a vertical on the circle several times each way to encourage the horse to land on the correct leading leg. Then I canter an oxer on the circle both ways.
- A favourite line of mine is two crosses 3 m to 3,7 m apart, then a vertical one short stride away.

Cantering the vertical fence on the circle

- When my young horse is quite happy with the above, I add a small spread, one or two strides away. Once he can manage that, I add a vertical one or two strides away from the spread. I play around with this type of exercise, using one to two strides between the fences after changing the verticals and spreads around.
- From the above exercises I graduate to jumping a vertical to oxer 1 m in height and with six to seven strides in between. This jump is placed in a straight line and I use the sand school, which is a restricted area of 29 m x 69 m. All my lines are jumpable both ways.
- Then I scale it down to four or five strides vertical to oxer and again oxer to vertical.
- Next could be vertical — one stride to oxer — four to five strides to vertical — one stride to oxer, jumpable both ways.
- The D Grade is now coping with spreads of about 1 m.

I would like to mention here that much of my time is devoted to riding the A Grades, to teaching and competing. Consequently, there are times when I don't ride a D Grade for a month and it is then that I rely upon an assistant to help me. My assistant undertakes the general exercising and fittening work. My assistants don't school the horses on the flat or over poles.

It will be nine months to a year before the horse graduates from D to C Grade (not including his first three months in the paddock) unless I feel he is thoroughly confident and has the talent to be upgraded earlier.

During his D Grade work, he will have been asked to change the rein from 20 m circle to 20 m circle using a simple change of leg. That is to say, I will have made the downward transition through four to six strides of trot before asking him to strike off on the opposite leg. Throughout this exercise, the horse must remain on the bit and make the transition fluently. He must also remain straight and he mustn't be allowed to swing his quarters.

By this time, the D Grade will have graduated to jumping 1,07 m at shows and he should be coping happily with his 1,15 m fences at home. Providing he is not rushing, hesitating or stopping, is capable of coping with the correct strides and distances and is having consistent, smooth, clear rounds, it is now time to opt him up to C Grade.

C GRADE

Once into C Grade, the horse is well on his way to being an A Grade, for in C, B and A Grade, he is going to be jumping exactly the same jumps he became acquainted with in D. However, these jumps will be higher, the related distances between them will differ and the angle of approach will vary so that the entire course becomes progressively more difficult.

For each grade, I use specific exercises and courses. The following ones relate to horses that have upgraded from D to C.

- I always trot any grade of horse into his first couple of jumps (always crosspoles) when warming up at a show. I follow this by trotting into a vertical at a height of 0,9 m to 1,14 m depending on the grade of horse. I then continue with my warming up at the canter over a vertical fence, after which I include a spread.
- When warming up at a show, I try to do as little as possible over fences so that I do not tire or bore the horse. One often sees people repeatedly schooling the horse over the warm-up jump; this is not its purpose. Racehorse trainers have a saying, "Don't leave a horse's gallop on the track" — it's in the race that you want the best performance. Likewise, don't leave your horse's jump in the practice arena; it's in the ring that you want him to give his best.
- At home, I nearly always start off with trotting poles into a vertical (the vertical with A Grades going up to a height of approximately 1,3 m). I also use several different gymnastic exercises; but my favourites (the ones I most frequently teach my pupils) are as follows:
  - Put trotting poles down to your vertical, which is 3 m away from the trotting poles. Then erect another vertical fence five or six short strides away, as shown in Figure 10.5. Ride this on six short level extra strides; when you can manage this, ride it on the correct five strides. When you try to ride this exercise on a short stride, you will soon find out whether the horse is balanced and obedient, especially when you push him on for the correct stride.
  - Turn the vertical into a spread and repeat the above exercise.

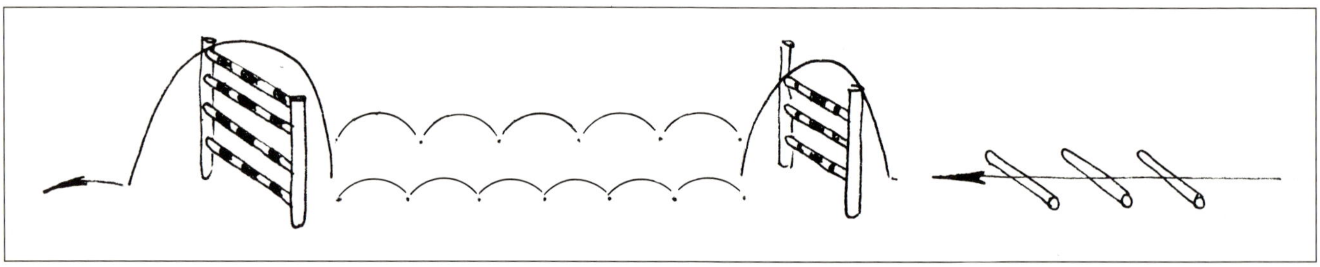

Figure 10.5

- You can enlarge on the above exercise by erecting two fences after the vertical. Erect two jumps, one to the left and one to the right, with only four, three or two strides between the

Figure 10.6

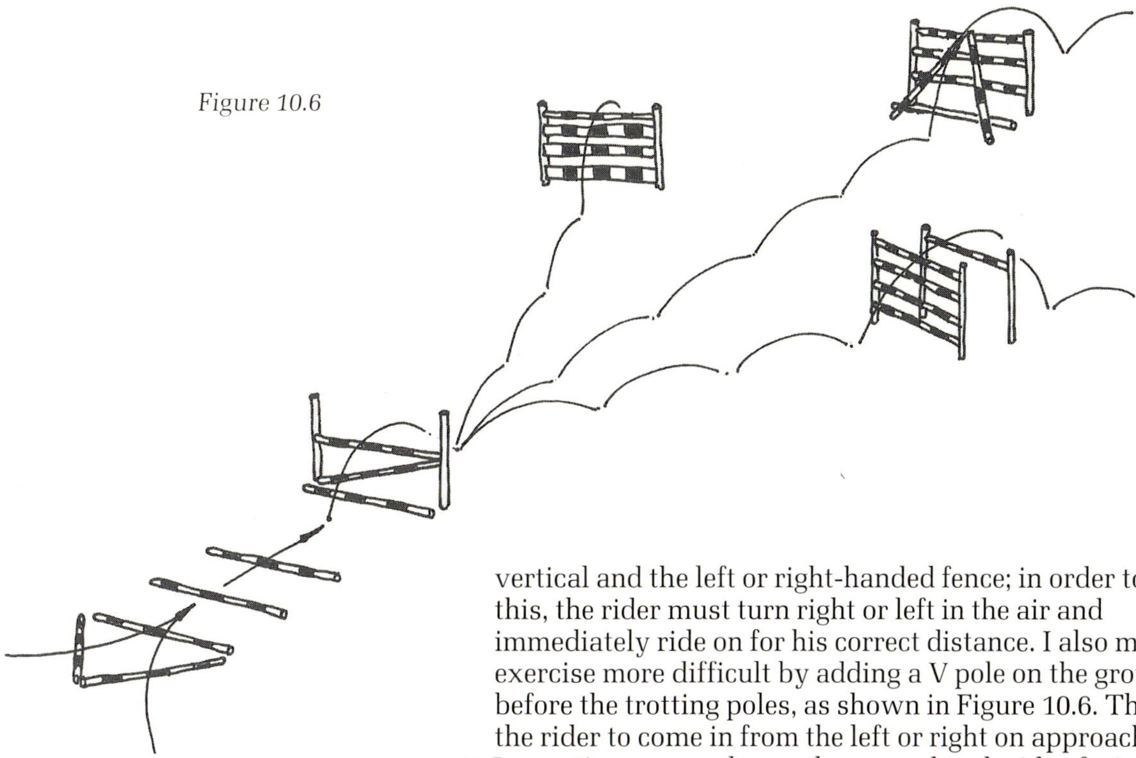

vertical and the left or right-handed fence; in order to jump this, the rider must turn right or left in the air and immediately ride on for his correct distance. I also make this exercise more difficult by adding a V pole on the ground before the trotting poles, as shown in Figure 10.6. This forces the rider to come in from the left or right on approach.

- I sometimes use poles on the ground each side of a jump, 2,7 m to 3 m away if trotting and 3,4 m to 3,5 m away if cantering. This exercise is really just to give the horse a correct takeoff and landing point when jumping and I use it mainly in the case of a horse that lands too far out over his jumps (in other words, when the apex of his jump is incorrect) as the pole on the landing side teaches him to pitch shorter (see photograph sequence below).

- From the above jump, I continue with a line of poles at 3,65 m intervals to a jump that may be five or six strides away (see Figure 10.7). This is an excellent exercise for a horse who has a particularly long or short stride. It helps to regulate the pace

Figure 10.7

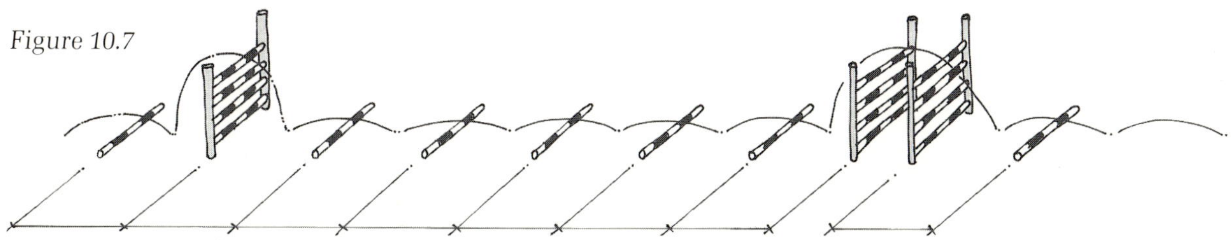

between the two obstacles without too much interference from the rider, as horses will avoid treading on the poles. (I use this often with jumps up to 1,4 m with my top A Grades prior to a big show.) The average horse's canter stride is 3,65 m.

- The picture shows a pole placed across the top of an oxer. This exercise makes a horse who tends to spread out and jump "flat" over a big oxer pick up his stomach and bascule.
- I would go so far as to say that V poles are one of my most commonly used exercises, and I use them for two reasons: to tighten the horse's knee action over the fence, and to help to stop a horse rushing his fences. V poles definitely teach a horse to back off his fences but I never use them without putting a takeoff pole on the ground 30 cm to 60 cm away from the jump.

- You can erect a course that has several different lines. It is a good idea to have at least five or six changes of direction in it. I have a particular course with 11 different lines and I build most of my jumps so that they are jumpable both ways. (This does not apply to a triple bar or a Liverpool type of jump.)
- In C Grade, the horse is introduced to a treble combination and I am careful not to overface the horse with heights or distances that he finds difficult to cope with. One of the easiest combinations for the young horse is a vertical to oxer to vertical, starting off with two strides between jumps and then progressing to only one stride in between.
- Another useful exercise is the vertical to oxer to vertical with three strides in between, or the same exercise but using three verticals three strides apart. By this time, I expect my horse to remain absolutely level between these fences.
- All my distances are standard:
  One stride = 7,3 m = 24′6 = 8 paces
  Two strides = 11 m = 35′–36′ = $11\frac{1}{2}$–12 paces
  Three strides = 14,6 m = 48′ = 16 paces
  Four strides = 18,3 m = 60′ = 20 paces
  Five strides = 22 m = 72′ = 24 paces
  Six strides = 25,6 m = 84′ = 28 paces
  Seven strides = 29,3 m = 96′ = 32 paces
  Of course, in a double, my single-stride distance is usually 7,5 m and between two verticals my distance for one stride would be 7,9 m. For a D Grade, however, I would keep the distance between two verticals at 7,3 m and for the real novice who is still trotting, at 6,4 m.
- At this stage, I start to jump the horse in my 1 ha grass paddock, which contains two water jumps, two ditches and two banks, and is not restricted in that there is no paddock

fence within four strides from landing. This makes the horse feel as though he has just been released from prison. As a result, he will often become a lot stronger between and after his fences, particularly if the paddock is on a slight slope (as mine is). A sloping paddock is a good testing ground for the horse's balance and for whether his homework has been done correctly.

- By now he should be well into C Grade, so I introduce him to water. A good size and shape for a water jump is 2,4 m x 4,6 m, as shown in the photographs.

- Put a pair of showjumping wings on the corner of the water jump. (If you don't possess proper wings, do as I do and use a 200 ℓ drum on each corner of the water jump with jump poles as wings.)
- I begin by emptying the jump of water and I then coax the horse to walk through the centre of it in both directions. After a couple of days practice, I put some water in the jump and I take the horse over it after getting a reliable and more experienced horse to give me a lead. Don't dismantle the wings just yet and, as a precaution, pop the reliable horse over the jump before trying to follow it on your inexperienced horse. The last thing you want is for the "reliable lead" to put in a stop and set a bad example to the young horse.
- I follow the lead four or five times and I then ask the young horse to jump the water on his own four or five times. When he has done this confidently, I put up a little brush box of 60 cm on the takeoff and give the young horse a lead again. Jump it four or five times until the horse is happy. If the horse is not getting enough height, build a little upright — just one pole about a quarter of the way in over the water — and this will make him jump higher. At some point, you must practise jumping a pole over water anyway because you'll find a jump like that in a competition sooner or later.
- Water can cause terrible problems so I always make *sure* I have taught the horse how to jump water before finding it at a show. If I were to find myself at a show where I was expected to jump water, I wouldn't dream of jumping it unless the horse was fully prepared. Fortunately, in C Grade, there is nearly always an option to the water, but if I were to enter a class on an unprepared horse and find that there was no

option, I would retire rather than risk shaking the horse's confidence.

- Don't think when you've jumped water at home once, that's it. It's not. Before every show where he will be expected to jump water, give the horse a reminder by practising at home. Don't go into the ring cold. (This doesn't apply to A Grades unless they have a problem with water.)
- It is worth remembering that the majority of real water stoppers are never cured. However, it is sometimes possible to restore the confidence of a horse that has had a fright. One of my A Grades, Country Cottage, had suffered a bad fright over water and I spent some considerable time coaxing him into it so that, in the end, he would stand in it quite happily. However, I wouldn't do this with a horse who wasn't afraid, otherwise he could just lose respect for water and start landing in it.
- Finally, never try to beat or drag a horse through the water. I have seen these methods ruin several good horses. Although you must be firm, do not resort to drastic measures; they don't work.

During the above training, the horse is usually well into jumping C Grade classes at local shows. I only travel the horse *away* to shows (as opposed to sticking to the local circuit) after he has spent three to four months in C Grade because it is expensive to compete a horse. Until you are sure he stands a chance of recouping some of the outlay by winning a class, you might as well stick to the local shows.

When a horse has only recently upgraded to C, I won't even consider jumping him against the clock. However, once he settles into the grade, I start to ask him to go against the clock — just to give him the experience of being pushed, more than anything else. I'm not really trying to win at this stage. In fact, it has never been my policy to push for first prize in the lower grades unless I feel the horse is 100% ready: often, you will find me jumping quietly round the jump-off in runner-up competitions to a Championship or Grand Prix. I prefer to save my horse for a full go in major competitions to the extent that, if I have a good horse, I like to be able to say, "that's the class I want to win."

I am happy to spend a year in C Grade but much depends on the horse. If he is doing four competitions a weekend, three weekends a month, in six months he should be ready to go into the next grade providing he has the talent for it.

FLAT WORK IN C GRADE To recap: while in D grade, the horse became established in his basic schooling. He was working on the bit, leg yielding, coping with travers and making smooth transitions up and down. He also learned to canter forward in a calm and balanced manner.

- It is now time to teach him to lengthen his stride along the long side of the school. I don't often ask a horse to extend "on the bit" because I prefer to use lengthening to encourage him to stretch his head and neck down and to stretch his back muscles (see photograph).

At this stage, I also start teaching the horse to do a flying change, in the following way:

- I have already asked the horse to canter diagonally across the school from say K to M, and as I approach X (which is the centre of the school) I squeeze him forward into a trot. I don't allow him to poke his nose or drop into a walk. After six to eight strides of trot, I ask him to strike off into canter, leading with the leg opposite to the one he was previously cantering on.
- Over a period of weeks, I slow the trot and also reduce the number of trot strides until the horse is coming back to trot, taking a couple of strides of trot, and then striking off into canter.
- By this time, I have started to collect the canter sufficiently to enable the horse to go from canter to walk. Once he has made the downward transition to walk, I ask him for two or three strides of walk and then I ask him to strike off from walk back into canter on the opposite leg.
- The flying change is a natural progression from the canter-walk-canter exercise, but certain things help to teach the horse to make that natural progression. I sometimes use the following exercise:
  — I canter (on the correct leg) up the long side of the school. At M or F, I make a half loop back to the long side so that I am now in counter canter. A couple of strides prior to meeting the fence on the long side, I put my inside leg (which has then become the outside leg) behind the girth. In the instant that I do so, I alter my weight, lift the horse forward with what is now the inside leg and when he changes leg, reward him.
  — A tap with the schooling whip behind the saddle on the outside will often help to make a horse change leg, but some horses may start to run away from the whip as a result, so this artificial aid must be used sparingly.
- When the horse is learning how to do a flying change, he will often disunite and some horses become excitable, trying to dash off. If this happens, keep the horse in a strong and forward-going canter and as he gets the idea, insist on his changing on the aid.
- Horses that are a bit slow in learning what is required of them might benefit from the following exercise:
  — Put a pole down at an angle to the long side of the school. Then canter along the long side of the school, round to A, and then make a half turn back to the long side of the school. By this time you will be in counter canter as you approach the pole. The horse is likely to jump over the pole, and as he does so, ask for the flying change. After a few attempts, the small jump he makes over the pole will then become a flying change. Eventually, you will be able to dispense with the pole altogether. I often use draw reins for this exercise in the begining in order to prevent the horse from running away from the leg and hollowing his back.
- In order to teach a horse to land on the correct leg, I approach a jump at the trot first, and when the horse is landing on the correct leg, I canter into it. If the horse is cantering on the right rein, he will be leading with his right foreleg. If, therefore, you

are cantering on the right rein and want the horse to land on the left leg in order to lead with the right foreleg, use your left leg strongly behind the girth when the horse is in mid-air over the jump. Do not over-use it on the takeoff, otherwise you will confuse and unbalance him. As you put your left leg behind the girth, put your weight to the inside (that does't mean ducking to the side of the horse's neck). The horse should now land leading with his right leg. Every time he lands and leads incorrectly, trot immediately (two strides) and change. When he does it correctly, reward him with a pat and the voice. Better still, if he lands incorrectly and if he can do a flying change, ask him for a flying change to put him back on the correct leg.

- The rein back. I used to be quite lazy about teaching my horses to do this. Then, about 12 years ago, the late Lachlan McLachlan's father Robert (an avid polo player) told me that in his field, he felt that a horse was never really obedient until he knew how to rein back on the aid. It doesn't matter how successful any of us are, we must always be prepared to listen to other people and to learn from them. As a result of what Lachlan's father told me, I have become a lot more conscious of the use of rein back in my schooling.

B GRADE

We have already said that as the horse upgrades, he is jumping the same obstacles, but they are higher. The related distances between them are more difficult and the angle at which he takes the jump may be more awkward.

In B Grade, the horse is expected to cope with heights of 1,3 m to 1,37 m, with spreads of about 1,3 m to 1,5 m. In other words, the jumps are 15 cm to 30 cm wider than those he met as a C Grade.

The following exercises relate to horses that have upgraded from C to B.

- You will often find four jumps at one end of my school, situated as shown in Figure 10.8. I use this exercise to test a horse's balance, turning ability and approach. In order to negotiate the jumps correctly, both horse and rider have a lot to think about: the rider must maintain the rhythm and remain on the correct line to each jump and he must ride the corners correctly and look to the next jump. The horse must land on the correct leg and remain straight until he has to negotiate the next corner. If the horse doesn't land on the correct leg, he must make a flying change on the aid. The rider must then place him at the correct takeoff point for his next jump. I often use this exercise with my advanced junior pupils.
- A figure of eight over a vertical jumped at an angle. The height of the jump should be determined by the ability, temperament and experience of the horse. Jumping a horse at an angle prepares him for the tight turns in the jump-off. It makes a

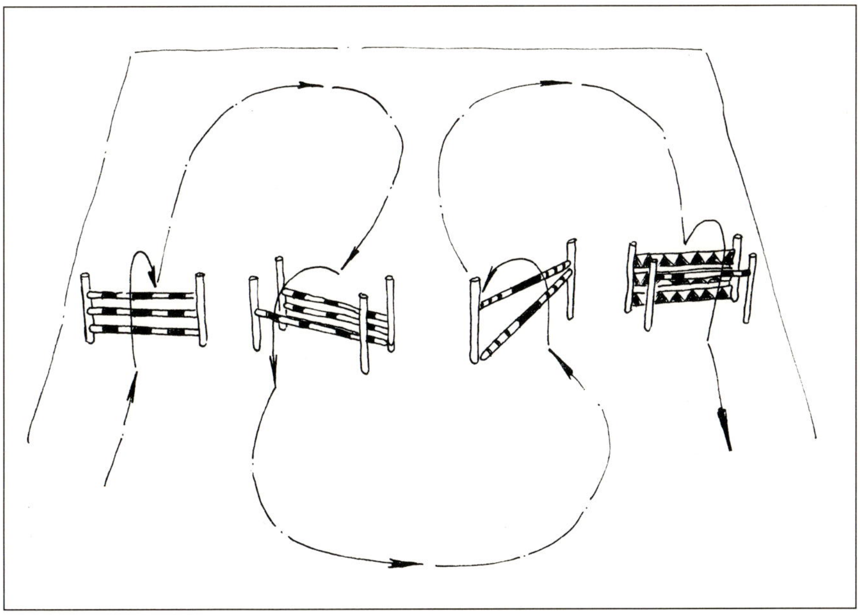

Figure 10.8

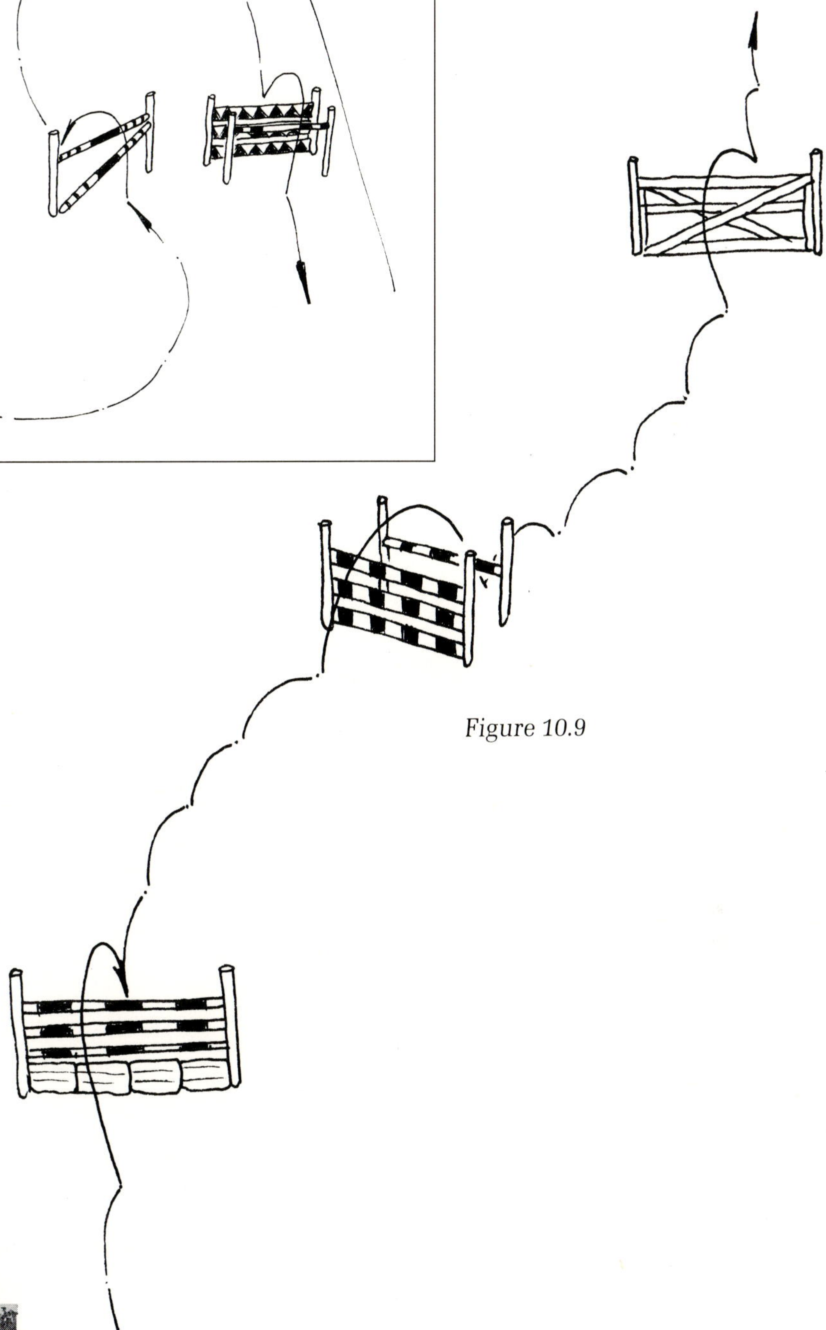

Figure 10.9

horse that tends to rush his jumps settle and it also helps horses that are slow in front tighten with their knees (see photograph left).

- Dog's legs, as shown in Figure 10.9. Again, the height and distance should be set according to the horse's ability, temperament and experience. I might have done this exercise in C Grade, but I concentrate on it more in B.
- I also work more on combinations.

FLAT WORK IN B GRADE

- Shoulder-in (at the sitting trot) on the 20 m circle: this is to supple the horse up and *keep* him supple. When I ask for shoulder-in, I ask twice on the left circle and twice on the right, and then I trot a circle with no shoulder-in to give the horse a breather before repeating the exercise. Be sure that the horse is going into the outside rein and keep your outside leg behind the girth so that you do not allow him to step out on the circle (which would render the exercise useless). The only way to achieve the desired result is repetition, correction and patience; but give the horse a break from time to time.
- The B Grade should be able to trot and canter on a long rein during his work programme. This is an exercise to encourage the horse to stretch his head and neck down. I want him to look as though he is going to eat grass at the trot. This exercise is excellent for his back.
- I ride a fair number of figures of eight at the trot and I also ride plenty of 20 m circles at the canter, asking for a flying change on each change of rein. At this stage in his training, the horse should stay on his hocks, must stay on the bit and must not fall to the inside or swing his quarters out. His change must be straight on the aid, with no quickening, stiffening or disuniting.
- You can now ask the horse for canter to walk to canter transitions; after this, you can ask for canter to halt to canter. In the strike-off, the horse must not throw his head up; he must stay on the bit; he must strike off from his hocks, and he must go forward into the bridle right on the aid. Make sure that he doesn't fall onto the forehand when you ask him to halt. If you don't ride the horse so that he keeps his hocks underneath him, he will automatically come down onto the forehand, which is the last thing you want. Nor must he fall behind the bit and give you the impression that he's collapsing behind; in short, the whole exercise must be in balance.
- Now that his work is fairly well established, after cantering a 20 m to 30 m circle on the right rein at one end of the school, make a downward transition to trot midway along the short side of the school. Three or four strides of trot will take you to the corner of the school and you can then ask for traverse down the long side. When you reach the corner of the long side of the school, make a half turn and at the next corner, strike off to canter on the left rein. Repeat the exercise.
- When doing the above exercise, I often use shoulder-in instead of traverse.
- The following is also a favourite exercise of mine: In sitting trot I turn down the centre line and leg yield to the long side. Once I reach the long side, I immediately change the leg yield into a shoulder-in and at the next corner, I do another half turn and repeat the exercise on the other rein.
- At this stage, I start half pass.

I feel I can demand a lot more of the B Grade which, at this stage, is well on his way to A Grade and should be executing the above exercises smoothly. They are an excellent test of whether he is working correctly and if he is, they will help him to reach the pinnacle of his showjumping ability.

Right: *Working a young horse on the flat*

A GRADE

This section deals not so much with the training of the A Grade (for he is already basically trained) but on treating him correctly and keeping him going.

When the horse upgrades from B to A, I normally keep him in medium classes for a year or more. During that time, he should gain confidence by jumping the smaller A Grade courses. He can then be asked to tackle more demanding competitions.

An exception to the rule was Watchfire, who had competed in only six shows as a medium A Grade before I travelled him to Cape Town for the Cape Protea International Show. At the time, my then top A Grade, Flaunt, was showing signs of feeling a splint he had developed, so I really put Watchfire in at the deep end by entering him for the Grand Prix . . . which, incidentally, he won.

After this show, Flaunt was operated on, so I kept Watchfire in the international classes, but I was careful never to overface him or get carried away in a jump-off and turn him too tightly into something that might rattle his confidence. Despite this, he went on to win the Tongaat Grand Prix, the Seiko Sun City Indoor Grand Prix, the South African Grand Prix, the Transvaal Championship, the Lowveld Championship and the FEI World Cup as well as the Showjumper of the Year award. However, Watchfire is not an average horse.

Perhaps the pressure of winning so many major competitions in his first year as an A Grade contributed to the unfortunate mishap we had at the 1990 Rand Show where in the Welcome Stakes at night he refused a jump at the last moment, hurling me face first into the top pole, smashing my right cheekbone in three places and causing a nasty gash. After eight stitches and reconstructive surgery to the cheek I was to sit out the Rand Show. Eight weeks later — my first time back on him — we won the Tongaat Grand Prix in fine style.

A Grades don't need to jump higher than 1,4 m at home. They already know their job and there is no point in wearing them out or boring them to death. My A Grades only jump once a week before shows unless I have a really good reason to jump more, but if a horse has been off work for, say, two months, I get him back on form by doing the following:

- Four to six weeks' fittening work by hacking him out, starting with light walking and trotting, until I have built him up to 45 minutes' trot and canter with only two short walks in between. Once the horse is fit, I find that 30 minutes' work per day is ample to keep him fit.
- Two weeks' schooling, the latter part over trotting poles and small jumps. (I don't do anything excessive in either the flat work or the jumping.)
- Once the horse is jumping fit, I progress until I am cantering him into a single vertical and oxer up to 1,2 m in height. During this phase I ask him to jump both the vertical and the oxer several times on each rein. Then, after a few sessions of

this (spread over a week or so), I ask him to tackle more demanding jumps and combinations.

The work I ask for depends on how the horse went at his last show. Horses pick up bad habits. If a horse knocked a brick out of the wall, put a foot in the water or dropped a pole on a particular type of fence, then that's what I work to correct. I bear in mind that sometimes I might be the cause of the problem; perhaps I'm doing something wrong. Sometimes, it's simply that the horse has started to bring his hind quarters to one side on approach or even over the jump. He could be jumping to the left or right, changing leg on takeoff, running into his jump or hesitating on leaving the ground. It may be that somewhere along the line he has lost a little confidence, and this can often be the cause of his developing any one of these bad habits.

A pole placed on the ground on the landing side of the jump to encourage the horse to remain straight over the fence

Speaking of bad habits, in 1979 I lost my first FEI because I had fallen into the sloppy habit of not holding my reins in a closed left thumb. I was turning sharp into a triple bar, which was the fourth to last jump, and the rein slipped clean through my fingers. I was so busy trying to correct my length of rein that I wasn't paying enough attention to the jump ahead, and Honey Girl hit the back pole. I was 27 seconds faster than the eventual winner, but allowing myself to slip into that sloppy habit cost me the FEI.

I rest my A Grades the week following a big show. For example, when Watchfire had jumped at the Derby for four days, which ended on a Monday, he was then off until Friday and I took him for a hack on Saturday and Sunday. On Monday he was lightly schooled on the flat, and on Tuesday he was schooled for 20 minutes. After the schooling session, I asked him to start off with trotting poles to a vertical several times after which he jumped a vertical fence a couple of times on each rein, then an oxer several times on each rein. To finish I went to a line at 1,3 to 1,4 m of a vertical to oxer to vertical with four strides between jumps. I put striding poles on the ground between the jumps and I asked him to do the jumps about three times each way. The parallel in that lineup was made absolutely square because he's an A Grade and he can cope with it. He then had Wednesday off because he travelled to Welkom. On Thursday and Friday he competed in the forerunner classes, and on

Saturday he won the South African Grand Prix.

Watchfire doesn't need a lot of work because he's a good horse that just needs to be kept fit and to be given the chance to keep his eye in. Had I been competing a horse with less ability, I might only have given him one or two days off and then I might have given him more work in the school, using different exercises to enable me to concentrate on whatever his weak points appeared to have been at the last show.

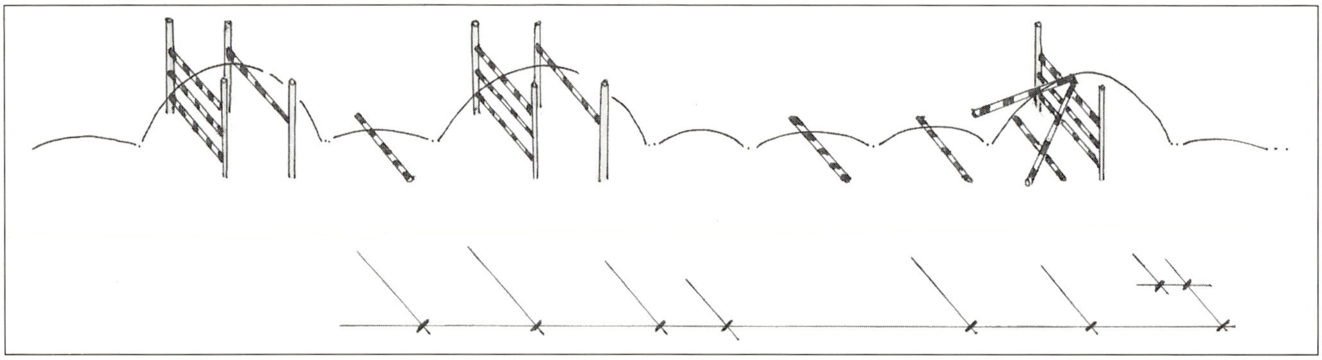

Figure 10.10

Lionel Dunning gave me the exercise shown in Figure 10.10, and I used it on Isis Bridge:

- Place two oxers 7,3 m apart at a height of 1,37 m square x 1,37 m wide.
- Then place a pole on the ground halfway between the two oxers, so that it lies in the middle of the horse's canter stride.
- A pole is then placed on the ground on the landing side, 7,3 m away from the second oxer, after which the next pole is placed 3,7 m away.
- This is then followed by a 1,37 m to 1,5 m vertical, which is again 3,7 m away and has V poles. Lying on the ground about 40 cm in front of the vertical is a take off pole.

This exercise was to make Isis Bridge stretch over two spreads and then balance himself up for his three strides to the vertical. The V poles kept him straight and tight in front.

The above exercise is *only* for A Grades and if you decide to use it, remember to make the fences smaller to start with, although the oxers can be widened to 1,5 m.

FLAT WORK IN A GRADE As we progress through the grades, we are constantly striving to improve our horse's flat work. By the time the horse is A Grade, I have incorporated counter canter into his schooling programme because it improves the quality of the true canter.

- I find the following a good exercise in counter canter: after cantering round the school in true canter, make a half turn back to the long side of the school. Do not change leg, but remain in counter canter. Go large and cut the corners. To discourage the horse from trying to change leg, keep your weight well into what has now become the outside stirrup and support him with the opposite leg by placing it slightly back against his side. Remember, do not try to bend him in the direction he is going. He must maintain the outside bend: he may be on a left-hand circle, but in counter canter; he must have a slight bend to the right, for his right leg is his leading leg. Once he can maintain his leg and balance, you can reduce the size of the circle until the horse can cope with a 30 m or 20 m circle in counter canter.

- I now want the horse to be capable of doing a flying change every four to five strides on the straight, as well as a half pass in canter. The latter I find useful when warming up before a big competition to sharpen him up to the outside leg in preparation for the turns he will meet on the course.
- The horse should now be capable of halting from canter, reining back four or five paces and striking off immediately into canter, and at this stage, he should be carrying himself with a nice springy stride.
- I do more long canter down the long side of the school and on 30 m or 40 m circles. I may have used running reins in the earlier stages of his training when he was in C Grade to help with this exercise but I should have dispensed with them by now. If I have any recurring problem with this exercise, I'll put the running reins on again to remind him. I want the horse to lengthen his stride and stretch his head and neck out towards the ground in much the same way as I asked for the grass-eating lengthening trot in C and B Grade. In A Grade, at the canter, his chin should be about level with his forearm, and to get him to do this, I half halt him and then squeeze him forward from my leg. I release the rein contact slowly, and I expect him not to run off with me or quicken his stride; he must only *lengthen* his stride. It is important not to lose the contact altogether. I do a lot of this exercise with Flaunt who is quite stiff in his back, although he does not appear so to those watching him jumping. I feel it is an exercise that gets a horse working through his back in a relaxed manner.
- In my 1 ha grass paddock, I expect my A Grade to come back to a collected canter after a fairly strong gallop three to four

Figure 10.11

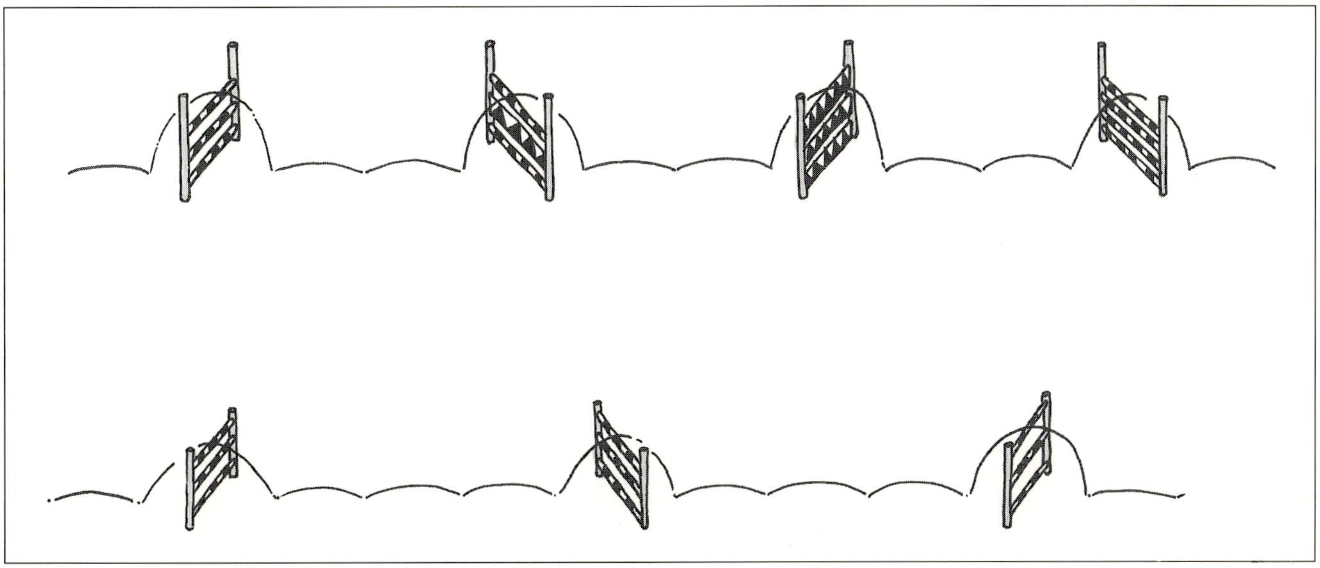

Pharaoh's Diadem jumps onto the bank at home, one of the many obstacles I use to train my horses

times around the field without any resistance to coming back to hand. In this gallop, the horse must carry himself and not throw up his head and try to gallop off (although he will probably be quite strong). In other words, I am looking for absolute obedience for my A Grade. I think it is good for a horse to have the odd gallop, providing the rider can prevent it from becoming uncontrolled. Even a sensitive, slightly hot horse (provided he's not too highly strung) benefits from this exercise because he learns that he can gallop without getting upset or trying to take control, and this helps for the jump-off against the clock.

- There is a speed class at Olympia where, amongst other jumps, riders can elect to jump a line of six jumps set at the angles depicted in Figure 10.11, with two strides between jumps. I have since used a similar exercise at home, but I use four jumps with two strides in between because my space is limited. This exercise is good for both horse and rider as it takes a lot of concentration from the rider and obedience from the horse. The best way to tackle this line of jumps is by taking a central line all the way.

11

WORKING AND RIDING THE HORSE

WORK ROUTINE

YOU'LL probably have noticed that I went on at length about the training of the D and C Grade and that, by comparison, I said little about training B and A Grades. I can only repeat what I said earlier: that the horse has learned basically everything he needs to know in D and C, and whether he reaches B or A Grade depends largely on:

- Whether the foundation work, be it flat work or jumping, was done correctly.
- The horse's physical ability, soundness and courage.
- The horse's temperament: he can have physical ability but if he doesn't want to do it, or he's afraid, he won't make it to the top.

So, once you get your horse to B and more particularly, to A Grade, his flat work should be designed to keep him supple and to remind him of what he has learned in the past few years. Also, remember that horses, as well as riders, pick up bad habits without really knowing they have done so, and these bad habits must be sorted out in the A Grade's schooling sessions. You don't need to keep training him as such — you just need to eradicate any bad habits that creep in, and keep him going in peak condition. In addition, the horse must be managed well in terms of feeding, shoeing and veterinary needs (I hope the subsequent chapters will offer valuable information on these aspects).

One of the things that will help to keep an A Grade at the top is a sensible feeding and work programme. Feeding the horse is dealt with in Chapter 13, and I shall discuss a basic work programme now.

- With the average A Grade, I often use one of the following work routines:

Monday — Holiday
Tuesday — Hack
Wednesday — Flat work. I will also jump him if his

performance at a previous show wasn't up to standard, and I would try to eradicate whatever the problem might be.

Thursday — The same as Wednesday
Friday — Flat work
Saturday — Show
Sunday — Show

Or:
Monday — Hack
Tuesday — Hack
Wednesday — School
Thursday — School and jump
Friday — Hack
Saturday — School and jump
Sunday — Holiday

Or:
Monday — Hack
Tuesday — School
Wednesday — School and jump
Thursday — School and jump
Friday — Hack or school
Saturday — Show
Sunday — Holiday

- It should be fairly simple for a thinking rider to put a work routine together. The hard bit is sticking to it and doing something when you don't really feel like it. I work to a routine throughout the grades and my routines don't vary all that much. I tend to follow the pattern below, unless the horse is going to a show:

  — D Grades sometimes school and jump up to four days a week (depending on the horse's needs and ability). In addition, they are hacked for two days and given one day off.
  — C Grades are schooled and jumped three (possibly four) times a week, hacked twice and given one day off.
  — B and A Grades are jumped only twice a week on average (depending of course on their show schedule).

However, there is always the exception that proves the rule. I have known horses that need to be jumped nearly every day if they are to perform to any standard, and I have known others that, once they know their job, hardly work over poles at all at home.

Right: *Watchfire*

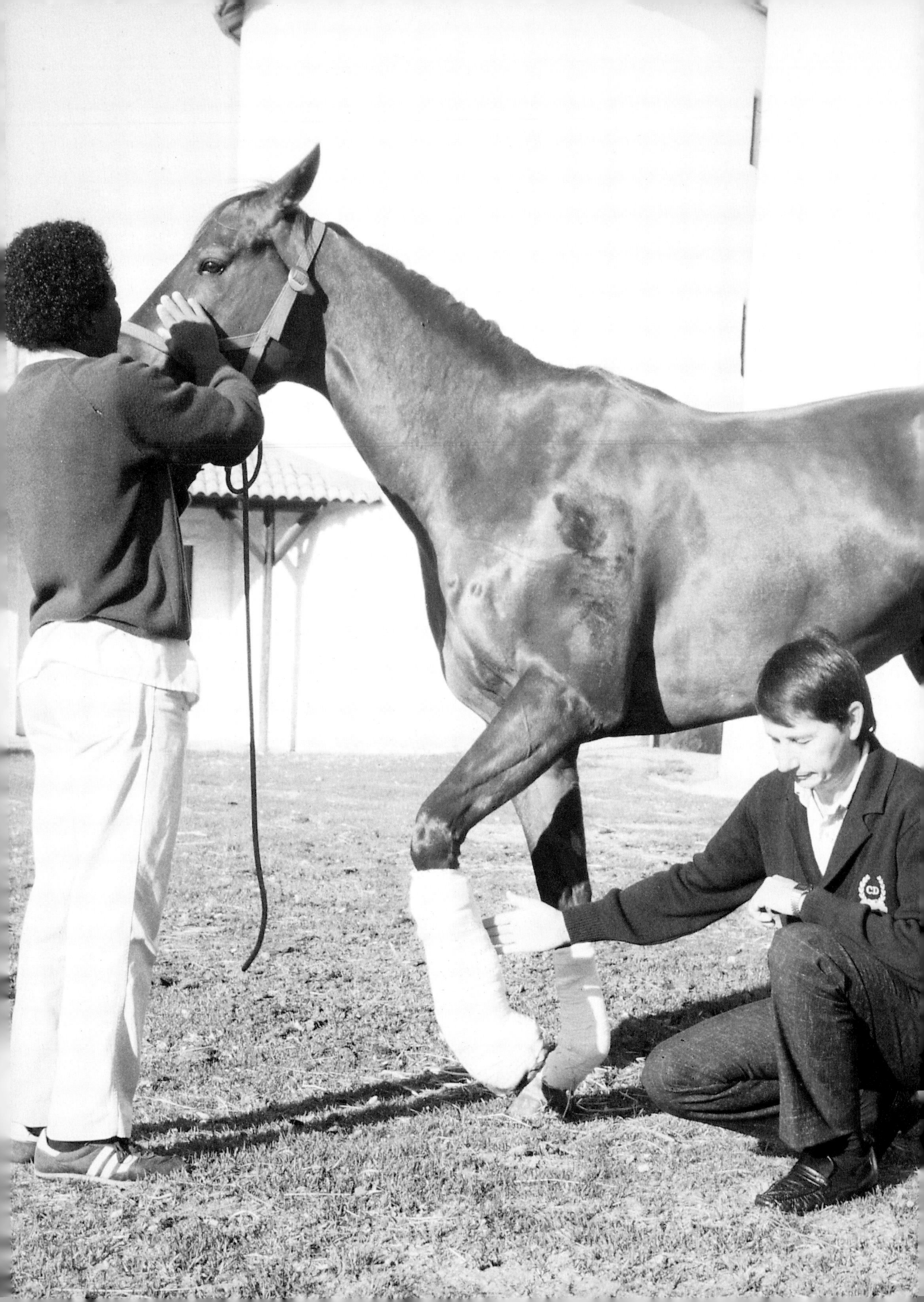
CD

12

A WORD FROM THE VET

by Dr André Rudolph B.V.Sc.

I CHOSE to hand the reins over to my vet and farrier at this point because the two sections were more informative when I allowed them to develop in this way. That was more important to me than having a book entirely to myself and I hope you will find their observations as interesting and helpful as I did.

Most vets will agree that some top-class riders have an instinct about their horses. It isn't always possible for them to tell a vet why they think their horse is ill when he appears to be perfectly well, and yet it will turn out that they are quite right. Gonda has very fixed ideas about most subjects relating to horses. She will spend half an hour telling the vet what is wrong with the horse so that the vet begins to wonder why he has been called at all.

I recall one particular incident when Gonda called me out because she thought Houselights was lame. Happily, I was able to tell her that on this occasion she was mistaken, but she disagreed and insisted he was lame.

As a matter of fact, Houselights had once had a tiny fracture at the bottom end of a splint bone, but this had healed long ago and I could find no sign of lameness as a result of it. Nevertheless, Gonda said she thought that the splint was worrying the horse and she insisted that I operate on it.

I said, "What must I operate on? The horse isn't lame, the X-rays showed nothing: I don't know where to operate!"

"Then do a nerve block."

I said, "There's no point if we can't see anything."

But Gonda insisted, explaining that she intended to ride the horse and *feel* whether he was better after a nerve block, so a deal was struck and, working totally blindly, I did it.

It turned out that Houselights improved when blocked over the original site of the fracture of the splint bone so I agreed to do an exploratory incision around that area. When I operated, I found that a piece of callus from the original splint fracture had grown and impinged underneath the suspensory ligament. This was obviously hurting him when he landed after jumping, and as X-rays are two-dimensional and can't pick up this sort of thing, it didn't show up. Needless to say, after the callus was removed Houselights returned to soundness and went on to be a top A Grade.

Apart from being able to feel when a horse isn't quite sound, Gonda's intuition is second to none: I clearly remember the time when Flaunt was suffering from lameness and, according to Gonda, required "urgent swimming". Fortunately, Gonda's intuition also told her not to swim him without a vet being present in case there was a problem of some sort, so she contacted me and requested my presence.

Flaunt was then shipped off to a neighbouring swimming pool where the manager was an experienced horseman, and after being kitted out in swimming tackle, he was coaxed down the ramp and into the pool.

All seemed to be going according to plan until, without any warning whatsoever, he went completely berserk. As a result, he lost all his swimming tackle and we were horrified when he suddenly slid sideways under the water and gracefully disappeared from view.

The water was the colour of pea soup and as we couldn't see where Flaunt was, we all just stood around the edge of the pool looking at one another in stunned silence. The seconds started to tick by ominously and I know we were all beginning to think he'd drowned. Then, quite suddenly (and just when we'd given him up for lost) two bright red ears and half a nostril appeared on the surface of the water swiftly followed by an extremely frantic Flaunt who was coaxed to the edge of the pool before being guided gently to land.

Fortunately, I had a tranquilliser at the ready but I was sorely tempted to give it to the onlookers since we were in a far greater state of shock than the horse.

Of course, it helps to take precautions against accidents and illness, and Gonda takes more than the average person, I think. She's the only person I know who has installed an intercom between the stable and the house so that she can pick up the sound of a colicky horse during the night.

One thing that Gonda has always been able to understand is that it's a rare vet who is truly incompetent: the exams are not easy to pass and it is rumoured that a vet has to have at least a modicum of intelligence to be accepted onto the course in the first place. Vets may not always succeed in solving a problem, but it's not for want of trying or training. Sometimes, when a rider has a run of bad luck and has a handful of horses out of action one after another, he's apt to blame the vet when, really, no other vet could have done better. A rider may then decide to change to another vet, which is a little unfair.

Working with Gonda has frequently been quite an experience, but she has rarely been unfair. Perhaps her extensive knowledge of horses has taught her that any of us can only do our best. At the end of the day the horse, his nature and the knowledge at our disposal will have the final say in the outcome whether we are jumping him or treating him for an ailment.

On the subject of ailments, I have outlined various problems below, believing them to be those the average showjumping rider is most likely to meet. However, when discussing treatments, I have merely given my opinion as Gonda's attending veterinarian and I have in no way intended to imply that the treatments I have recommended are the best; merely that they are the standard.

It seemed sensible to start by discussing what stress injuries the average racehorse may already have when we purchase him with a view to making a showjumper of him. I then move on to specific lamenesses, common ailments and problems associated with the horse's back as I feel this gives an overall view of the problems most frequently seen in the average showjumping yard.

BUYER BEWARE!

Since most showjumpers in South Africa are inherited from the racetrack, most potential showjumpers therefore start their career with varying degrees of body wear and tear from their racing careers.

Fortunately, this type of wear and tear usually relates to galloping and it affects the body differently to the wear and tear induced by showjumping. Consequently, there is seldom a compounded strain and one may largely overlook many racing problems.

Some classic examples of the wear and tear one can expect to find in the ex-racehorse are:

- Arthritis of the knees and fetlock joints. This is very common with racehorses and yet some showjumpers have been known to succeed competitively for many years without constant medication for this problem.
- Hock trouble affects racehorses and showjumpers equally, for both suffer a similar strain behind.
- Wind problems affect showjumpers less than racehorses because the oxygen required by a showjumper is far less than that required by a racehorse.
- If a showjumper is blind in one eye, the disability is more serious than it would be in a racehorse. However, horses have been known to jump successfully at a high level with vision in one eye only. If a horse's eye is affected by retinal atrophy he may have only partial vision, and this can lead a racehorse to shy from vaguely seen obstacles. As a result, he may be a hazard on the racetrack. It is sometimes safer to race a horse that is completely blind in one eye than to race a horse with one eye partially blind. However, this is not the case when

riding a showjumper. It has been known for a totally blind horse still to do dressage in a controlled situation but to do anything further with it would be dangerous.

- Horses frequently suffer heart strain after they have been raced excessively, but if they are given a reasonable period in which to recuperate, they often recover to showjump without risking the safety of the rider. However, any heart problem must be investigated by a vet to assess whether there is a risk.
- Horses are frequently warned from racing because they suffer nosebleeds. The source of a nosebleed could be the nose itself, e.g. an ethmoid haematoma. This is serious in that only major surgery will correct it. If a horse bleeds from the lungs, it tends to be a recurring problem, but it is less serious in a showjumper because the bleeding is minimal. Horses may also bleed from the guttural pouch — a serious condition. A diagnosis is made by looking down the nostrils with a light called a laryngoscope.
- Anabolic steroids are prohibited substances but in certain countries are still used in racehorses to enhance the metabolism and promote stamina and endurance by their hormonal effect. These substances are known to be addictive in humans; they are also addictive in horses, so that when a horse ends his racing career and no longer receives steroids as a showjumper, he may show a decline in enthusiasm and condition for several months after racing. Fortunately, this is reversible in that the horse will simply recover eventually although he will of course suffer withdrawal symptoms: losing condition and becoming listless.

LAMENESS AFFECTING SHOWJUMPERS

The first thing to discover is which leg is lame, and we do this by trotting the horse out. The vet doesn't watch the horse's legs in the hope of discovering where lameness is present; he watches the horse's top outline, for this will enable him to detect which limb is lame.

LAMENESS OF A FRONT LIMB

When a sound horse trots, his head moves parallel to the ground without nodding. If he is lame in one of his front legs, the head will dip when the *sound* leg strikes the ground. This action gives

Figure 12.1
Lame near fore

rise to the statement that a horse raises his head when the *lame* front leg bears weight (see Figure 12.1).

LAMENESS OF A HIND LIMB

Lameness in the hind leg can be detected when the vet watches the horse's quarters as the horse is trotted away from him. In a sound horse, the quarters dip normally as each hind leg bears weight, but if one hind limb is lame, the quarter will dip *more* on the side in which the lameness is present (see Figure 12.2).

Figure 12.2
Lame off hind

FINDING THE SEAT OF LAMENESS

Having decided which limb is lame, the next thing to discover is where exactly the site of pain lies. The vet will start by examining the hoof, and from there he will work his way up the leg until he discovers the seat of lameness.

LOW HEELS

Thoroughbreds trained to race often have low heels because they have been shod with a type of shoe designed to enable them to reach their full speed potential. This puts a strain on the navicular bone. In extreme cases, low heels can even *cause* navicular disease.

CONTRACTED HEELS

It is not inadvisable to purchase a horse with contracted heels provided an X-ray is taken to eliminate bone conditions such as navicular disease.

BOXY FEET

A boxy foot usually develops after a young horse has been overfed. This leads to low-grade laminitis, which changes the shape of the foot.

LAMINITIS

This extremely painful condition is caused by:
- Overfeeding;
- Concussion;
- Drugs;
- Fever (the result of an infection);
- Retained afterbirth.

Laminitis (see Figure 12.3) is easy to diagnose since the horse stands with all four legs slanting forward and he is reluctant to move, particularly if he is asked to move sideways. In severe cases, the pedal bone rotates as a result of laminitis and this is difficult to correct (see Figures 12.4 and 12.5). However, once the

Figure 12.3

pedal bone has stabilised in a new position, the rotated pedal bone is best left alone. In a mild case of rotating pedal bone, the horse may still be salvaged as a jumper, but he will need a good farrier for the rest of his life. The farrier should not be tempted to trim the sole of a horse with a rotated pedal bone, because there is insufficient protection between the sole and the ground, and to trim the sole would further deplete this protection.

If a horse has had laminitis as a foal, it does not usually become a recurring problem, but if a horse gets laminitis as an adult, he is prone to relapses.

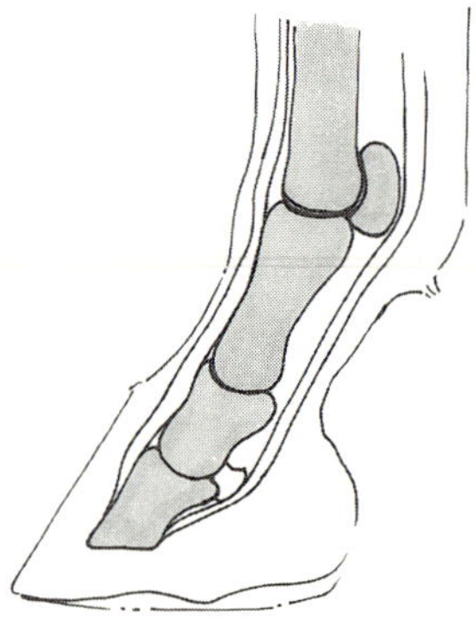

Figure 12.4

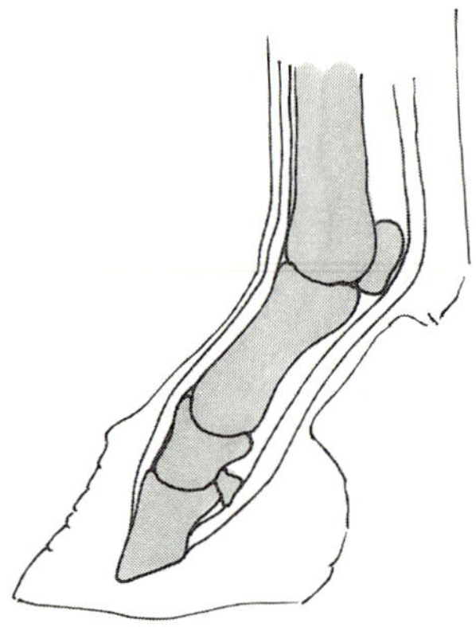

Figure 12.5

12.4: *Normal pedal bone parallel to hoof*
12.5: *Pedal bone beginning to rotate with laminitis*

TREATMENT

- The best treatment for laminitis is to eliminate the cause.
- Magneto pulse (providing it is started immediately) on a frequency of 17 has proved to be a help to the horse suffering from laminitis, because this improves the blood supply to the hoof before the cells have a chance to die off.
- Painkillers are essential, but it is wise to avoid cortisone.
- Endotoxin antiserum and drugs affecting anaerobic bacteria can be useful in the acute stage.
- Drugs that improve the horse's circulation.

Good management of a horse prone to laminitis is essential if the laminitis is to be prevented from recurring.

SIDEBONES

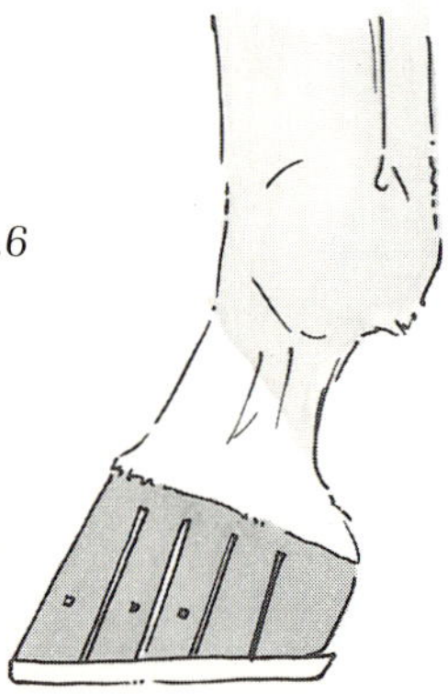

Figure 12.6

On the hoof are two cartilages, one on each side, which sometimes calcify and become sidebones. More common in warm-blooded horses than in thoroughbreds, they are sometimes caused by the foot not being shod level. Although the reason that sidebones sometimes calcify is not always known, certain types of hoof conformation predispose the horse to sidebones. Sidebones are easy to diagnose if large, when they can be felt as firm areas above the quarter of the hoof.

TREATMENT

The best treatment is for the vet or farrier to groove the hoof which will allow the hoof to expand away from the bone and reduce the pressure (see Figure 12.6). Once they settle down, sidebones rarely cause a problem, but some hooves have to be grooved throughout the horse's life to reduce pressure.

NAVICULAR DISEASE

There are different types of navicular: some forms are caused by injuries; some by excessively low heels; another type is linked to the blood supply in that bone. It is important to be aware of this when purchasing the horse because many horses suffer from a mild form of navicular disease. However, if the horse is an A Grade, providing the navicular is mild, the horse may still be worth purchasing. However, such a horse would need careful monitoring and treatment if necessary, so an experienced vet must be in regular attendance.

SYMPTOMS

- The main symptom of navicular disease is usually a very mild lameness; sometimes the horse will warm out of it. The lameness comes and goes over a period of time, but the horse is always lame when trotted on a firm surface in a short circle.
- Some two-year-olds show severe symptoms and then grow out of it for a while. Then, as the horse grows older, the navicular pain may recur with milder symptoms.
- If a good horse becomes a "stopper" (providing of course that he is in the hands of a capable rider), it's a good idea to check that it isn't navicular disease making him unwilling to jump. The pain he feels on landing is sufficient to discourage any horse. If ridden by a capable rider, a novice horse that is stopping is suspect for the same reason.

To help him effect an accurate diagnosis, the vet may use:

- X-ray;
- Nerve block;
- A test involving hyper-extension of the foot.

TREATMENT

- The vet may use a drug that will dilate the arteries and improve circulation to the navicular bone.
- Certain drugs, which were once used to thin the blood and enable it to reach the affected part, are now out of favour. They are considered too dangerous since they may lead to internal haemorrhage.
- Shoeing the horse with a raised heel will help in some cases.
- A painkiller is indicated.
- Magneto pulse may be used to advantage in certain cases.
- Neurectomies have been performed for many years, but this operation may be banned in future in an attempt to eradicate navicular disease as a hereditary condition. The operation is simply the cutting of the nerve that supplies the navicular bone. Often, after a period of two years or more, the nerve can reattach and become sensitive again. After surgery to cut the nerve, a neuroma (a painful nerve ending) sometimes develops. If this happens it is advisable to resort to ultrasound therapy as a means of desensitising the neuroma, for an attempt to remove the neuroma by operating is often futile and may in fact risk the strangulation of the blood supply to the hoof due to scar tissue forming around the closely lying artery. This can cause the hoof to slough and the horse will then have to be destroyed.

PYRAMIDAL DISEASE

Pyramidal disease is a fairly common complaint, especially in its milder form where a small piece of bone is chipped from the top front end of the pedal bone, often in both front feet. It is usually caused by injury. If the fracture is large, the hoof will grow away from the fracture or chip and will become shaped like the bow of a ship. Very tiny chips can be just as serious as bigger chips, if not more so, because they can be squashed into the coffin joint where they may cause severe lameness.

SYMPTOMS
The horse may be perfectly sound at times and acutely lame at others.

TREATMENT
It is difficult to operate: the area is surrounded by hoof and largely inaccessible. The prognosis is therefore guarded. However, grooving the front of the hoof will sometimes alleviate the problem instantly.

RINGBONE

A ringbone is a growth of bone around the pastern area. It often results when a horse sprains a ligament after turning sharply on one leg. It is important to realise that the condition can easily be misdiagnosed initially because it can take up to six weeks for the calcified area to develop sufficiently to show on an X-ray. Therefore, if an X-ray is clean but lameness persists, a further X-ray should be taken six weeks after the first in order to ascertain whether ringbone is the cause. If the horse is not rested, ringbone gets worse, and it therefore naturally follows that the condition is made worse if the horse is lunged. Some horses jump successfully for years without pain and a horse with ringbone is therefore not always a write-off. The vet is able to assess whether the ringbone is likely to settle or get worse on radiographic appearance.

SESAMOID LIGAMENT SPRAIN

The sprain of the ligament that attaches to the base of the sesamoid bones is caused by the horse putting his foot down awkwardly and injuring himself as a result. Fortunately, this is an easy condition to diagnose because the affected area is situated just below and on the sides of the sesamoid bones and is painful to the horse when palpated.

TREATMENT
- Rest and anti-inflammatories. If the horse is not rested and treated, he may develop a large lump of bone below the sesamoids, which may result in a more serious lameness.
- Laser.
- Magneto pulse.
- Pin-firing.

SESAMOIDITIS

This condition is the result of injuries sustained during racing and can also be caused if a horse is worked excessively when immature. It occurs in the two small bones behind the fetlocks and is fairly common. However, it is seldom a problem in showjumpers unless there are signs on a radiograph of the suspensory ligament having been torn from the sesamoid bones, in which case one must be wary of sesamoiditis.

TREATMENT

- The horse should be rested to allow the suspensory ligament to reattach to the sesamoid.
- Pin firing is commonly used as a method of treatment.
- Immobilising the leg in a plaster cast and using magneto pulse is helpful in a severe case.

SPRAINED SUSPENSORY LIGAMENT

This condition is not commonly found in showjumpers, but when it does occur, it requires extensive rest in addition to whatever treatment is advocated by the vet. One sometimes discovers a very inconspicuous swelling where the suspensory attaches to the sesamoid; as mentioned under *sesamoiditis*, this can be very significant.

TREATMENT

- Rest
- Anti-inflammatories
- Laser
- Pin firing.

HIGH SUSPENSORY DISEASE

The name of this condition is misleading as it is not a disease at all: it appears to be a sprain of the suspensory where it passes between the splint bones just below the knee. This is one of the most common causes of intermittent lameness in performance horses.

SYMPTOMS

- The symptoms are characteristic: the horse is very lame for a few strides, but at other strides he is not lame at all (as opposed to: sound one day, unsound the next). The horse is usually also lame on a circle.
- Symptoms can persist for years if the condition is not positively diagnosed by injecting local anaesthetic into the actual ligament to see if the lameness completely disappears. This condition is difficult to diagnose positively if a vet uses a nerve block to help him in his diagnosis: the horse might be sound *purely* because he is going through a sound period, and not because the site has been nerve blocked. Consequently, this condition causes a great deal of controversy until it is successfully diagnosed.

TREATMENT

- Anti-inflammatories or laser; pin firing is also effective.

FETLOCK JOINTS

It is fairly common for a vet to see a lot of wear on the fetlock joints of a racehorse. This wear is not so common in a showjumper unless he was previously a racehorse. To assess a fetlock joint, feel the texture of the joint and beware of any joint that feels asymmetrically rough or knobbly on the surface. Reduced flexion (which can be the result of adhesions around the joint without involving the joint itself) isn't necessarily a problem, providing the bones of the fetlock joint are all right, and this can be seen on an X-ray.

TREATMENT

- Drugs injected into the joint for persistent lameness.
- Surgery can be used to remove small chips and nodules.
- The annual application of a working blister may benefit the horse showing joint wear.

WINDGALLS

There are two types of windgall. The first is a swelling of the joint capsule or of the tendon sheath, and the condition is only termed "windgall" if it is not associated with lameness. This type of windgall may be drained for cosmetic reasons.

The second type of windgall is very firm when palpated and is associated more with scar tissue than fluid.

Windgalls are often caused by a tight annular ligament over the joint and this can cause severe lameness which may have to be corrected surgically. Physiotherapy, like ultrasound, will remove scar tissue.

SPLINTS

Splints are associated with young horses but they may well occur in an older horse. When growing, a splint can cause temporary lameness and if the splint is low down, it can impinge on the suspensory ligament and cause permanent lameness. Nevertheless, splints are usually overrated as a problem: people are wary of them simply because they can see them. They are caused by injuries to the splint bones which grow small calluses on them as a response to the injury. Soft bones are predisposed to splints, as are legs set "off the mid-line". Most splints are calluses, which round off with time and get smaller. Various remedies are credited with speeding this process.

TREATMENT

- If splints are to be removed surgically, it is best to give them time to stabilise first so that there is less chance of their recurring.
- Massage with various gels can help over a period of time.

TENDONS

Tendon injuries are common in showjumpers and are usually caused by an overreach injury. This is why it is important to put both tendon and overreach boots on performance horses. Bandages do not afford sufficient protection. If a tendon has been severed by a hind hoof, it can be diagnosed by running one's finger down the tendon: if there is a dent at the site of the overreach, this injury is very serious and will lead to a bowed tendon (see Figures 12.7 and 12.8).

TREATMENT

It is advisable to operate on tendon ruptures and such operations must be followed by a lengthy convalescence.

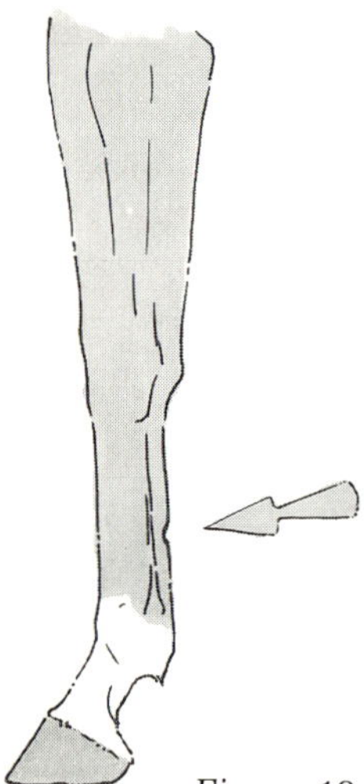

Figure 12.7

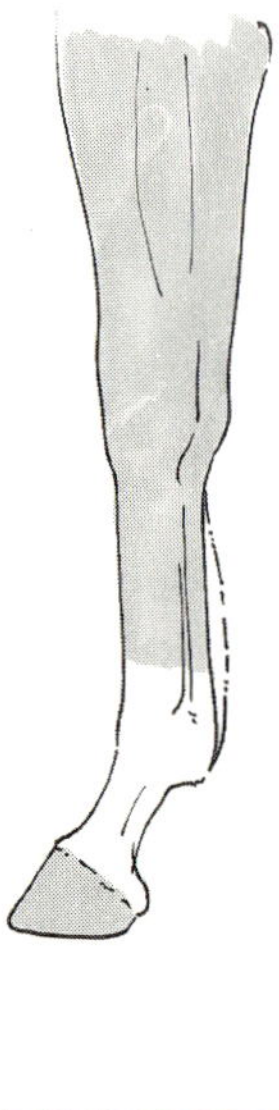

Figure 12.8

BOWED TENDON

This condition is frequently seen in old horses where the unfitness of the animal causes his muscles to work out of rhythm to the opposing pull of his mass on the tendon. The tendon cannot take this stress and bows as a result (see Figure 12.8). It is worth remembering that the horse might not go lame unless pushed to the limit, and if the bowed tendon is the result of an old injury, it usually settles well enough to enable the horse to continue to jump, providing the injury was not too severe in the first place. However, if the bowed tendon results in a great deal of scar tissue around the tendon, the horse is at risk of repeatedly breaking down.

TREATMENT

- The treatment of a bowed tendon is controversial: sometimes the severity of the injury is misinterpreted because the amount of swelling does not always correspond to the amount of torn fibres. Only scanning the injury can give an accurate assessment of the damage. Once this has been done, carbon fibre implants, laser treatment, anti-inflammatories or poulticing may be recommended. Beware magneto pulse, since this can give a false impression of recovery by merely reducing the swelling.
- A method of inserting carbon fibre implants has been developed as a result of work done in various countries: a large trocar is inserted down the middle of the damaged tendon and a strand of carbon fibre is pushed through this trocar into the required place. The trocar is then removed, leaving the fibre in place. Shortly after the operation the bow starts to straighten, after which the tendon appears completely normal. This method is effective because the carbon allows the blood supply to penetrate the centre of the tendon and heal it, which would not normally happen if the horse was left to heal naturally. If a careful work programme is restored over a period of nine months following surgery, the prognosis of this type of operation appears to be excellent.

KNEES

If the knee appears to be the site of lameness in a horse that was once trained for racing, look for tiny swellings on the front of the knee joint. These swellings might be small chips and could be more serious than large swellings, which are usually caused by the horse knocking the jumps. Knee chips are almost never caused by jumping, but by fast gallop work.

Sometimes you will see a swelling that looks like a capped knee. If you push on it, you will notice that the fluid goes up the side of the leg where the tendon is; this is a tendon sprain and needs to be treated differently to a capped knee.

TREATMENT

- Knee chips require surgery.
- Big knees can be drained or blistered if recurring.

ELBOWS

A horse rarely suffers lameness stemming from the elbow. It is a stable joint anatomically, but it can sometimes have congenital bone cysts. Fracture of the elbow or olecranon, which is the part of the elbow, usually occurs when the horse tries to rise after falling.

TREATMENT

- If there is no displacement of the fractured bone, this injury has a good chance of recovery.
- If there is displacement of the bone the injury requires surgery.

SHOULDERS

With regard to the shoulder area, remember that if the horse is sore in the foot, he often gives the appearance of being lame in the shoulder because he may trot out with a shouldery action. This leads to many lamenesses being attributed erroneously to the shoulder. Lameness in the shoulder can be due to a bone cyst or to injuries of the joint or biceps.

TREATMENT

The shoulder sometimes responds well to ultrasound treatment, irradiation or intra-articular injections.

The **hind leg,** up to the hock, suffers from the same injuries as the front leg, with the exception that ringbone of a hind limb has a better prognosis than ringbone of a forelimb. The same is true of splints, which are less serious in a hind limb than in a front limb.

BONE SPAVIN

Classically a bony lump just below the chestnut, most bone spavins are not visible except on X-ray. The lameness resulting from a bone spavin is often caused by poor conformation where excess strain is placed on the inside of the hock; it can also be caused by an injury. Bone spavin, a form of arthritis, is shown up when the leg is flexed and released immediately prior to the horse being trotted up in hand. Called a bone spavin test, this also shows up lameness in the stifle or fetlock, so don't automatically presume a bone spavin is present if the test is positive.

TREATMENT

Surgery is usually successful; pin firing and magneto pulse therapy are also used, as well as anti-inflammatories. The horse should normally be kept in light exercise for this type of arthritis: rest usually does not help the problem.

BOG SPAVIN

A bog spavin is a swelling of the hock joint capsule. It's easy to see and some people therefore confuse it with a bone spavin. It is characterised by a swelling in front of the hock and can be caused by a sprain, poor conformation or a degenerative disease. If the horse is not lame on flexion, disregard the bog spavin as a potential source of lameness, but X-ray the horse for a condition called osteo-chondritis dissicans (OCD).

TREATMENT

- Swelling can be drained for cosmetic reasons.
- OCD lesions are best treated surgically.
- Rest will allow a sprained hock joint to recover.

THOROUGHPIN

A thoroughpin is a swelling of the tendon sheath just above the hock and it is caused by a sprain of the tendon in that area. It seldom causes lameness but if lameness should occur, the hock should be drained and treated with anti-inflammatories or hyaluronic acid. Raising the horse's heels with navicular pads helps to alleviate the problem.

RUPTURE OF THE FIBULARUS TERTIUS TENDON

This tendon joins the stifle and hock so that if one bends, the other must bend also. If this fixed ratio is disturbed (as was the case when Honey Girl caught one of her hind legs in a back pole) the tendon, which lies in front of the leg, will tear. A rippling of the achilles tendon behind the leg will indicate this injury.

TREATMENT
The tendon can be repaired surgically, or the condition may recover if the horse is rested.

STRING HALT

This is an exaggerated flexion of the hock. The cause is unknown. Horses with this condition can still jump, although they look awkward: string halt is a good example of a leg that looks lame but isn't lame at all. The fact that the horse isn't lame can be detected if the vet looks at it from behind: the horse doesn't alter his quarter when the legs bear weight.

TREATMENT
String halt can be corrected surgically as long as there is no concurrent bone spavin.

THE STIFLE JOINT

This is a common site of lameness. The cause may be that the horse has injured himself, for example by rising to his feet in the box; OCD or bony cysts may also be the cause. Stifle joint lameness can look similar to hock lameness. In order to ascertain whether the stifle joint is the site of lameness, the vet will palpate the joint slightly for any sign of swelling.

TREATMENT
- If the stifle has been injured, inject the joint with an anti-inflammatory drug.
- If OCD is present, surgery can be attempted.
- Irradiation will often help for recurring lameness.

LOCKING STIFLES

This condition is a dramatic sight: the entire leg, bar the fetlock, becomes totally rigid. The condition is probably hereditary and is often detected when the horse is less than two years old. It is usually only seen after the horse is stabled without exercise for a couple of days, and it is this "standing in" that brings locking stifle on. This is because the stifle ligaments shorten while the horse stands, with the result that the patella becomes locked over the ridge of the femur bone.

TREATMENT
- First unlock the stifle: with the palm of the hand, push the horse's kneecap forward and inwards. Thereafter, shoe with

wedges on the horse's heels and give the horse as much exercise as possible once the stifles have unlocked.
- If the stifle locks repeatedly and severely, surgery is recommended. The required operation can be performed under local anaesthetic.

THE HIP JOINT

The hip joint is sometimes injured, as a result of which the horse will trot with his leg turned out at right angles to his body, even when the injury has settled. He manages well in a paddock if arthritis is not severe.

BACK PROBLEMS

The horse's back is a vital part of his locomotive system, and yet remarkably little attention is paid to its function and potential or actual problems. The entire area, from poll to tip of tail, is often completely overlooked because the symptoms of a bad back are frequently insidious.

Detecting symptoms of a back problem is not an easy task: the horse suffering from a bad back often still performs. The showjumper, for instance, will still jump; the racehorse will still race; but whatever his discipline, the horse will not perform to his full potential.

Before we look at how a back problem can be detected in a showjumper, let's turn our attention for a short while to the racehorse, because his predicament gives a good illustration of how difficult it can be to detect a sore back.

A racehorse with a back problem may typically perform so well on the training gallops that his trainer justifiably expects him to win when he is actually raced. However, contrary to all expectations, the horse fades during the race and is unplaced.

The trainer is perplexed. He orders blood tests and may even revise the horse's feeding or training programme. The blood tests indicate that nothing is amiss. Because the horse continues to train well, the trainer becomes seriously worried after he continues to perform badly when actually raced.

What has happened is that the horse is suffering from a back problem that does not trouble him severely enough to affect his performance on the training gallops. However, when the horse is being raced under maximum pressure, the extra tension and strain put greater stress on the back — and he fades.

If such a racehorse is treated there is a marked improvement in his performance. The improvement is easier to measure in the racehorse than in the showjumper.

SYMPTOMS

- When the horse is walked out in hand, he may sway behind or look a bit wobbly on his legs. The extent of this unsteadiness behind will depend upon the severity of his back problem and the horse's reaction to it.
- If a horse is trotted up in hand, an observer will not see

anything amiss unless the horse has a sensitive spot just behind the base of the withers. A sensitive spot there will cause him to trot or canter "short", and he will also shorten his stride when asked to canter.

- When a rider mounts a horse with a back problem, the horse may or may not buckle under the rider's mass. If the horse buckles but appears sound after the rider warms him up, he is said to have a "cold back".

People are quick to notice when a horse is lame from a leg problem but an equal degree of pain resulting from a back problem is not so easily seen. Fortunately the horse does give us other indications of back pain, providing we know what we're looking for: the showjumper may start to crash through his fences instead of clearing them and/or he may adopt a hollow outline. (Bear in mind that some successful horses jump with this style quite naturally.) (See Figures 12.9 and 12.10.)

Figure 12.9

Horse well rounded over fence

Figure 12.10

Horse jumping hollow

Figure 12.11

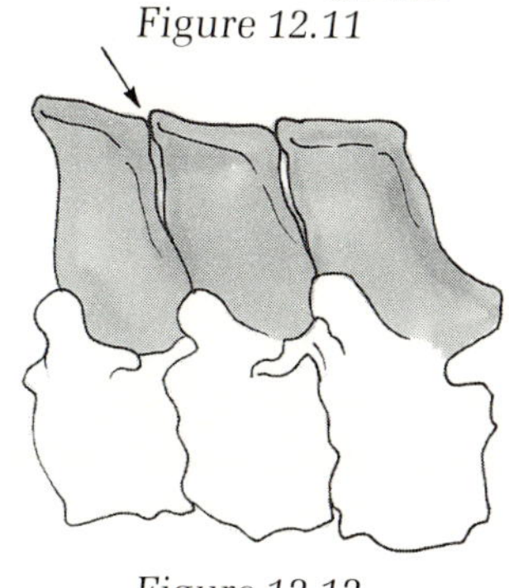

Figure 12.12

What happens is that as the horse lifts off, he feels pain. This pain is sometimes caused by a narrowing of the spaces between the vertebral spines (see Figures 12.11 and 12.12), causing the bones to be pinched. Ironically, when the body feels this pinching, the strong back muscles tighten up to immobilise the vertebrae and this causes the bones to pinch even more. So, at best, he flattens over the jump; at worst, he crashes through it.

DIAGNOSIS

If a horse has shown any of the above symptoms, the vet can diagnose the site of pain by palpating the back. To do this, he runs his fingers down the mid-line of the dorsal spines of the vertebrae, that is, exactly down the centre of the back. It sounds a fairly simple procedure, but one needs a certain amount of experience before one can tell whether the horse is moving away because he's ticklish, because he's being awkward, or because he's feeling pain.

When palpating a sore back, check that it is not merely the skin covering the vertebrae that is sore. An ill-fitting saddle can bruise the skin, causing severe discomfort to the horse. If the skin is sore but the saddle fits well, it is possible that the horse has hurt himself, perhaps by rolling in the paddock.

A ticklish horse soon stops moving away from the vet's hand if he is being gently palpated. However, if the horse is in pain, he will keep on moving away from the vet's hand. With experience, a vet can soon discern whether there is a problem, and if so, where that problem is located.

The mid-line should be checked first, because this is usually the primary site of pain. We refer to muscular discomfort as a secondary site of pain because the muscles surrounding the spine are tense and sore from the burden of trying to prevent the vertebrae from moving. If the problem with the spine is alleviated, the muscles relax of their own accord.

When a sore back is suspected, it is good policy to X-ray the spine to see whether there is any closing of the gaps between the vertebrae (we call this "kissing spines"). If nothing is visible on the X-ray, one of the following possibilities may be causing the pain:

- The ligaments of the spine may have become sprained.
- The horse has extremely sensitive skin. A poorly fitting saddle can cause considerable discomfort. Such a problem is easy to detect, because the horse will be reluctant to let you even groom the part of his skin that has become sore. It is a superficial pain.
- Although the muscles are normally regarded as a secondary site of pain, it is possible that a pulled or bruised muscle may be causing the discomfort.
- Spondylitis is another cause of a sore back, but it is rare and quite difficult to diagnose. A horse suffering from this condition will have a very painful back and will show lameness in his hindquarters.

Other problems that can mimic back pain are:

- Wolf teeth or cheek teeth with hooks (see Figure 12.13) can make a horse jump in a hollow outline. This is because hooks hurt the mouth when the bit pushes the cheeks against the sharp edge of the teeth, and to evade the pain, the horse will throw his head up and arch his back.
- Some hind limb lamenesses can make a horse tense in the back.
- Trainers and owners will frequently suspect that a horse has sore kidneys when in fact the horse is suffering from a back problem. Painful kidney disease is uncommon in horses and the signs are similar to mild colic rather than pain in the back. The kidneys and back muscles can become painful following a bout of azoturia. Here the mid-line spine should not be sore but the muscles on each side of the back will be in painful spasm.
- It is worth remembering that a horse can also suffer a sore **neck**; such a horse will be reluctant to do anything. When he walks, all four legs will be stiff, and he might not even want to eat. Sore necks frequently result from a badly sited injection or one that has caused irritation to the neck muscles.

While discussing necks, we come naturally to the wobbler syndrome: a wobbler suffers a restriction of the spinal canal, but his main problem is that his neck articulations degenerate, leading to arthritis of the vertebrae. It is hard to diagnose a

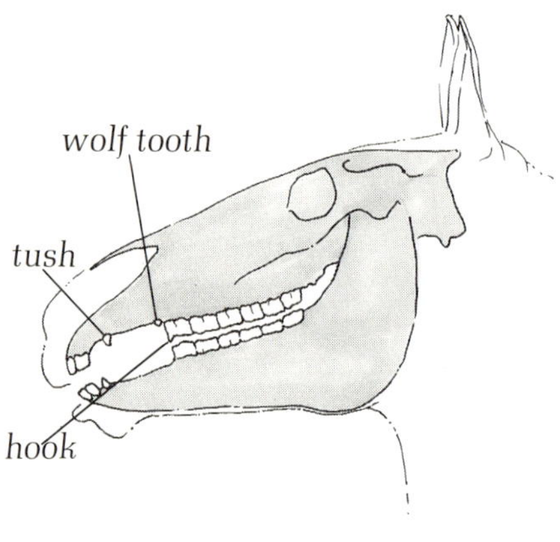

Figure 12.13

wobbler, but as the name suggests, he wobbles, and this condition can be slight or severe. In slight cases it can be detected only in the hind legs, but in severe cases it can also be seen in the front legs. However, it is not usually as severe in the front legs as in the hind.

The condition affects the balance of the horse but is not usually painful. It is usually detected when the horse is a two or three-year-old. It is important to check every young horse for this condition because even an extremely mild case can cause considerable trouble and frustration to the horse's owner. Having said that, I know of a case where a horse raced until he was a five-year-old. He won three races and was then sold as an eventer. His new owner complained he couldn't get the horse to collect properly, and the horse was subsequently diagnosed as a wobbler.

Withers virtually never worry a horse, except in the following cases:

- If the saddle fits incorrectly it can cause a pressure sore.
- Fistulous withers is an infection of the bone and surrounding tissues.
- The horse has reared over backwards and fractured his withers. This type of injury usually heals spontaneously.

Another injury that affects horses is a sprain of the **iliosacral joint** near the quarter. This is the result of the pelvis tearing away from the spinal attachments, and it usually occurs only on one side. This injury can be seen by the vet when he stands behind the horse: one pelvic bone is higher than the other over the centre of the spine. A fresh injury can definitely affect the horse's performance. If, however, the site of the injury is palpated and found not to be sore, the vet can be fairly confident that the injury is old and that it will not be of any consequence to the horse. Horses can even jump successfully despite this injury.

The **tail** of a horse is not significant in so far as back problems are concerned. Even if a horse were to lose his tail for whatever reason, he would still be able to jump as before.

CONFORMATION

While it is obviously wise to buy a horse with a short strong back, one should not be put off a horse who has a sway or roach back providing there is no evidence of pain: I have seen sway and roach-backed horses jump A Grade courses. Ideally, though, a horse should have a back that is not too long, and a purchaser should steer clear of a horse whose back is weakly coupled to the hind limbs.

COMMON PROBLEMS

BILIARY

The seriousness of this tick-borne disease can sometimes be overrated: it rarely causes death in horses. It can affect the heart and vocal cords but it is unusual for it to cause permanent heart damage if it is treated early.

AFRICAN HORSE SICKNESS

This disease manifests in late summer and is caused by an insect-borne virus, which has nine strains. The midge picks up this virus from an unknown source. The disease does not manifest in the midge breeding season; it is seen later when midges are plentiful. Unvaccinated animals contract three types of the disease; if not treated, young horses can die within a couple of hours of contracting it. Being an insect-borne disease, it doesn't spread from horse to horse directly. It can be prevented by annual vaccinations.

In South Africa, stabled horses rarely contract the disease. In fact, racehorse owners don't vaccinate, not because they are reckless, but because there is an old theory among trainers that vaccinated horses don't perform well. This has no scientific basis. Trainers rarely see the disease because their horses are stabled.

TREATMENT

Reduce the horse's blood pressure. Remove his water for about two days and administer anti-inflammatories and diuretics. In acute cases, treatment is not very successful.

NON-SWEATER OR ANHYDROSIS

This is a disease of unknown cause, which frequently occurs in horses that have moved to a humid climate where they ought to sweat more than normal. Of horses shipped to Central Africa, 60% develop this problem; 1% of those shipped from Europe to Durban develop anhydrosis. It is also common in horses shipped to India for polo.

If the body cannot sweat, the horse's temperature rises and he becomes extremely uncomfortable (and badly behaved). The rider may not notice that the horse isn't sweating and discipline him. Instead the horse should be cooled down by hosing. This method can effect a cure if it is applied every time the horse is worked. In fact, non-sweaters sometimes cure themselves over a period of years.

SUMMARY

It wasn't possible for me to incorporate every problem that might affect a showjumper, nor to cover the problems in any real depth. However, I hope that what I have outlined above will give you some idea of the extent and variety of the problems a vet sees most frequently in a showjumping yard.

Right: *Honey Girl*

13

SHOEING THE SHOWJUMPER

Andrés Canovas

DURING the 17 years I have been a farrier (eight of them spent shoeing Gonda's horses) I have had the opportunity of observing factors that have a marked impact on the feet and shoeing of South African showjumpers: the extensive use of thoroughbreds (of which the majority come from the racetrack), extremes of climate, hard ground and the problems resulting from these factors.

Much of the literature on shoeing which is available to the South African rider has been written by European and American farriers for European conditions, so it does not always relate to local conditions. For this reason I have covered some peculiarly South African factors in this chapter.

Although the horseowner cannot be expected to be an expert on his horse's feet, I believe it is essential for him to understand the principles that govern horse shoeing. Such an understanding will enable him to recognise his own horse's particular needs, to co-operate with the farrier and to distinguish good and bad workmanship on his horse's hooves.

However, this chapter is not to be regarded as a definitive treatise on farriery but rather as a reference for the everyday problems facing the showjumper and his rider.

With regard to the horse's feet, it is vital for the owner to work together with the farrier and the vet. Each has a contribution to make, and one may identify a problem area that has escaped the other's notice.

THE HORSE AS AN INDIVIDUAL

Each horse is an individual — a fact I cannot emphasise too strongly. I shoe approximately 100 horses a week, and no two horses are the same. In fact, not even a horse that appears to have four matching feet has even two hooves the same. It is therefore necessary to assess each individual hoof of each horse and to shoe it according to its own merits and failings.

There are certain ideals to which one can aspire, but always look at your horse within the wider guidelines laid out here. That way, you will not feel that your horse is abnormal; nor will you have unrealistic expectations of your vet and farrier.

Always work with the horse and his advantages, minimising any shortcomings, but never work against his natural make-up.

THE OBJECTIVE OF SHOEING

The purpose of shoeing is not forcibly to mould the horse's foot into a theoretical ideal, but rather to look at the foot within the framework of the demands made on a showjumper. One must then work within that framework to cater to the horse's needs.

The intention is to keep the horse sound for as long as possible while enabling him to withstand the stresses and strains of extended periods of showjumping.

THE FOOT IN MOTION

For the horse to remain sound, the ideal action of the hoof in motion, irrespective of gait, is a "clean" action.

The horse should move perfectly straight with hooves coming down heel first, then breaking over at the centre of the toe. (This is known as the break-over point.) There should be no sideways rocking movement as the hoof lands.

The following are important about the break-over point:

- A horse's foot follows the path of least resistance. As the foot comes down to earth, the heels make first contact, after which the foot comes down flat. It then rolls over onto the toe and leaves the ground.
- Ideally, the break-over must be quick, as this offers the least resistance and minimises strain on the ligaments and tendons of the leg.
- Horses with long toes and a resultant slow break-over break down more readily than horses with a rapid break-over.

THE IDEAL FOOT

To understand the problems that arise when a foot is less than perfect and to appreciate the corrective action to be taken, it is

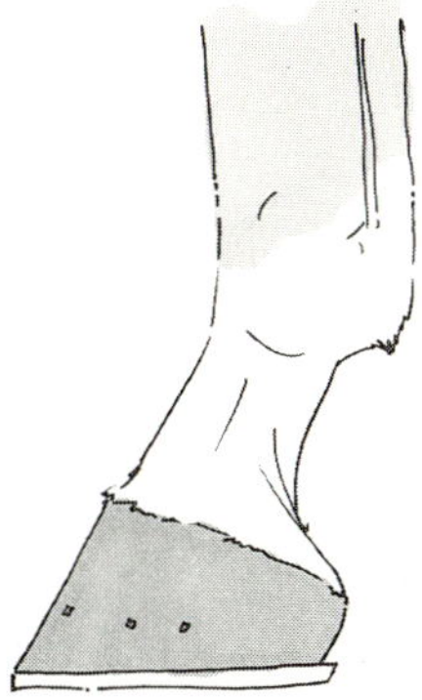

Figure 13.1

necessary to know the "ideal qualities" desirable in the foot of a showjumper:

- A broad, open foot.
- Good quality of hoof, with walls that do not crack when nailed because they are pliable and able to "give" in work.
- The angle of the hoof and the pastern should be the same.
- Underneath the foot, the bars should be strong, the frog well developed and the sole firm.
- The hooves must be proportionate to the size of the horse.
- Good heels, which can take the mass of the horse without being worn away disproportionately to the toe. The length of the wall from the coronet to the heel should be as close as possible to a third of the length of the wall from the coronet to the toe. Remember here, however, that one cannot insist on adherence to a mathematical rule while ignoring the practical reality of the living horse, which is subject to many variables.

SPECIFICS OF SOUTH AFRICAN SHOWJUMPING

YEAR-ROUND JUMPING

There is no break in the South African showjumping season. It lasts the entire year, and the only respite some horses can expect is the rest given when they are undergoing their horse sickness inoculations.

Such a programme results in the horse's legs and feet being in constant work and therefore in constant wear. Not that this is necessarily a bad thing: a correct feeding, work and shoeing programme can keep a horse that is constantly in hard work in top condition. However, it is worth bearing in mind that if a horse is bored with his work or tired as a result of it he is more likely to injure himself.

EXTREMES OF CLIMATE

All horses (whether in year-round work or not) are affected by a climate that can alternate between exceptionally hot and wet and cooler and very dry. Such a variation in climate can, and often does, have an adverse effect on the hoof. This is because water is an essential component of the wall of the hoof and moisture must be retained if flexibility is to be achieved and maintained.

The moisture level in the hoof is variable. There can be either an excess or a lack of moisture depending on contributory factors:

- The vascular system supplies the hoof with moisture from within while the insensitive components (the wall and the sole of the hoof) absorb moisture from the ground and the atmosphere.
- The moister air of the rainy season is, in general, beneficial to the hoof: in the majority of cases, hooves grow more rapidly in the rainy season. This can result in a reduction in the horse's shoeing cycle. Nutritional and hormonal influences during summer also affect hoof quality and growth.

An excess of water results in the following:

- Hooves become too soft and their walls therefore break easily.

- Walls crumble away and are difficult to nail.
- Frogs soften, which increases the likelihood of the sole being bruised if the horse steps on a stone.
- In the case of an unshod horse, the hooves may wear away extremely rapidly.
- Owing to the softness of an over-moist foot, grit may enter through the whiteline and travel up into the hoof, causing seedy toe and infection.

When a foot is too moist, one or all of the following actions can be taken:

- Hot shoe the horse in order to seal the foot.
- Keep the horse on dry bedding. (Sawdust helps to dry out the hoof.)
- Do not put the horse out into a waterlogged paddock.

If your farrier or vet considers that despite the over-moist condition of the hoof, a hoof dressing is necessary, add a third Stockholm tar to the hoof oil and remember that one should never apply Stockholm tar to the coronet as this causes blistering.

In the dry season, the reverse situation applies. The parched ground and air absorb moisture from the hoof so that it dries out. The following can result:

- The hoof becomes hardened; it loses elasticity. In some horses, the foot becomes very brittle. The foot shrinks: in some cases, the horse takes a shoe as much as one full size smaller during the dry season.
- Contraction and concussion.

Contraction does not merely mean that the hoof gets smaller; it is a specific condition in which the foot becomes narrower. The frog then tends to shrink; it fails in its function as a shock absorber and this can lead to corns, lameness and an increase in concussion. A horse suffering the above will be reluctant to move out freely.

Concussion occurs when, as a result of the hoof's drying out, it no longer expands and contracts as it should. At its extreme, this condition causes the horse to become hoof-bound, which means that the outside hoof presses on the soft tissue within, much like a person wearing a shoe a size too small.

For all the above reasons, a dry hoof has a greater tendency to vertical cracks than does a moist hoof.

The remedy for dry hooves is to replace the lost moisture, and one replaces moisture not with oil, but with water, because hoof oil cannot add moisture to a foot. It can only seal in what is already present. Furthermore, hoof oil will prevent any moisture from an outside source from being absorbed. Therefore:

- Allow the bedding to remain moist. This does not mean allow the horse to stand in bedding soiled by urine; it means moisten the bedding with water.
- Whenever you can, put the horse where his feet are surrounded by moisture. For example: when the horse is hosed down after work, leave him standing in the water or make a water patch where the ground is saturated, and tether him there for a period each day. The hoof is hygroscopic which means it has the ability to absorb moisture from the environment.

EXTERNAL FACTORS THAT AFFECT THE HOOF

FEEDING

"You are what you eat" is a maxim applied to humans, but it applies equally to all animals. If the horse's diet is deficient in certain nutrients, that deficiency will often make itself apparent in the condition of the horse's hooves.

If an apparently healthy horse has weak hooves (and if his weak hooves are not a condition to which he is genetically predisposed), then a dietary additive is likely to benefit him. The good commercial brands available all contain specific amounts of minerals, trace elements and vitamins, and these are an excellent supplement to the horse's basic diet. However, they cannot be considered a cure-all for weak feet.

BEDDING

The amount of moisture in the bedding will affect the moisture content of the horse's hooves.

Moist bedding, however, must not be confused with dirty bedding. If the bedding smells of ammonia, it must be considered dirty. Ammonia attacks the periople (the natural protective coating on the hoof wall) and destroys it, leaving the foot open to excessive moisture gain or loss.

Dirty bedding also heats up through spontaneous combustion, and this heat provides the ideal condition for the development of thrush, a necrotic infection of the frog.

HOW THE HOOVES ARE CLEANED

The hooves need to be cleaned not only underneath, but also on the outer wall.

The continuous application of hoof dressing builds up a film consisting of alternate layers of hoof dressing and dirt. This film covers the periople and unless it is removed by a weekly cleaning with warm water and a hard brush, the periople will ultimately be destroyed. Once this has happened, the wall will become "cheesy" and it will then crumble away.

When cleaning the underside of the hoof, the instrument used must reach deep inside all crevices. Most thrush occurs when hooves are cleaned superficially with little effort to investigate and clean out the deep narrow areas around the frog.

DRESSING THE HOOF

A hoof in good condition needs little dressing. The hoof wall grows down from the coronet and the coronet can be kept supple with a good hoof ointment if required. Stockholm tar should never be applied to the coronet as this will result in blistering. Hoof oil does not agree with all horses: some react badly to oil applied to the hoof wall, and this becomes apparent when the hoof begins to crumble. If your horse's hooves react badly to hoof dressing, either do not use a dressing at all or, if you believe that some form of dressing is necessary, dilute the hoof oil with a third Stockholm tar.

FREQUENCY OF SHOEING

A shod horse does not wear away his hoof by natural abrasion and the wall needs to be trimmed regularly if the hoof is to remain healthy and on the correct axis.

The hoof fibres point forward. As the hoof grows, the tendency is for the toe to grow longer; which results in an alteration of the angle of the hoof, and a subsequent broken axis between the pastern and the hoof.

The longer the toe, the more difficult the break-over, the greater the stress placed on ligaments, tendons and joints, and therefore the shorter the effective life of the showjumper.

Most showjumpers are shod every four weeks. There is no doubt that by leaving the horse for five or six weeks between shoeings, the working life of the top competition horse is shortened because he will, invariably, ultimately develop leg problems.

A horse competing in a competition four weeks after being shod should be shod again the week before the show in order to shorten the hoof before he competes. This will not harm the horse's hoof, providing the hoof is in reasonable condition.

The shorter the hoof, the less the stress on the foot and limb, and also, the less chance there is of the horse injuring himself.

AMOUNT OF WORK BEING DONE

The more a horse works, the more the circulation in his hooves is increased. This results in the hoof growing more quickly than it would otherwise have done, which necessitates a shorter shoeing cycle.

SURFACE ON WHICH THE HORSE IS WORKED

The surface of the arena in South African yards is usually either sand or turf, or a combination of sand and sawdust.

A sand arena can have two distinct effects on the hoof of a working horse: firstly, the abrasive action of the sand can wear away the periople, the consequences of which have already been discussed; secondly, that same severe abrasive action can wear away the sole of the foot.

A thin sole evidences itself as follows:

- The horse will go sound on hard ground, but in the arena he will be tender-footed. This is because the sole has been eroded to such a degree that the sand of the arena (which tends to pack into the foot regardless of whether the sole is eroded or not) exerts pressure through the sole against the soft tissue within the foot. Consequently, the horse feels discomfort every time he puts his foot down on sand (but not on hard ground, for hard ground cannot pack into the sole). Bruising may result.
- This condition is almost always confined to the front feet and seldom affects the hind feet. Far more weight is borne on the front feet, which carry the head and neck. To rectify the problem, the horse should have a full pad on the front feet between shoe and hoof to protect the sole and to allow it to build up again.

In some sand arenas, there are horses that may wear the toes of their hind feet away — even to the sensitive laminae — by coming down toe first. The solution here is a shoe with a broad heavy clip at the toe.

FACTORS SPECIFIC TO EACH INDIVIDUAL HORSE

CONFORMATION

Gonda comments earlier in the book that she would buy a ewe-necked, sickle-hocked, calf-kneed monstrosity if it was a proven winner that hasn't shown a day's unsoundness.

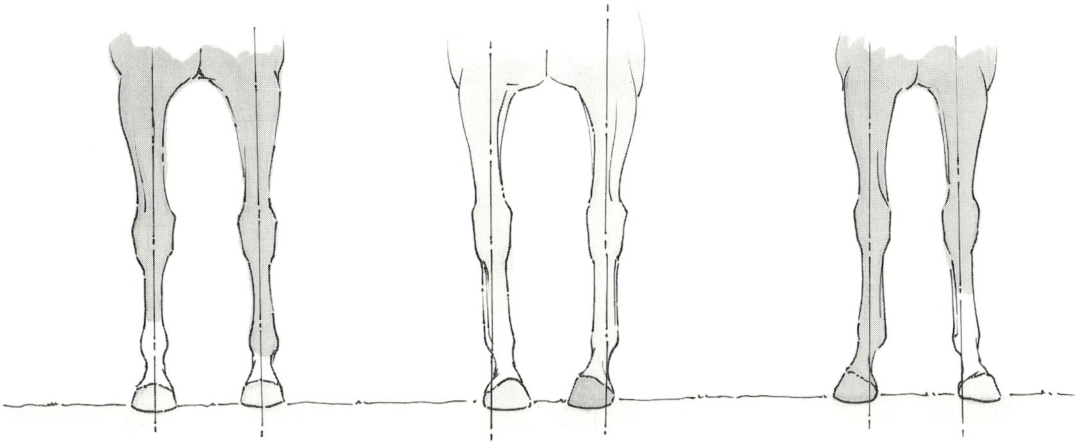

Figure 13.2

Conformation, and how the "good" and "bad" points are combined, directly affect a horse's movement and ultimately the manner in which his hooves come into contact with the ground. The better a horse's conformation, the more likely it is that his foot will attain the ideal of flat contact on landing, and the higher the likelihood of his remaining sound throughout his career.

Although we try to make the horse's hooves *look* as good as possible, the single most important contributory factor to keeping him sound over a long period of time is to ensure that he hits the ground level with all four feet, at any gait.

The lower down on a horse a deviation occurs, the easier it is to correct through shoeing.

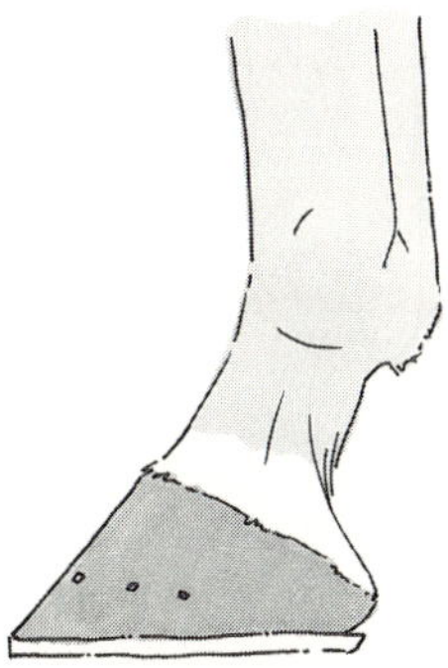

Figure 13.3

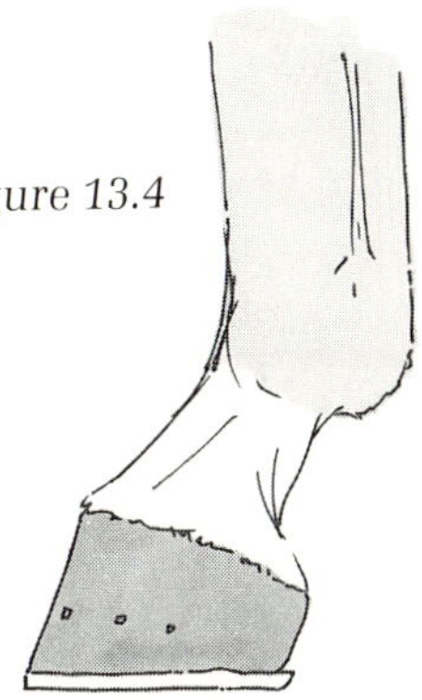

Figure 13.4

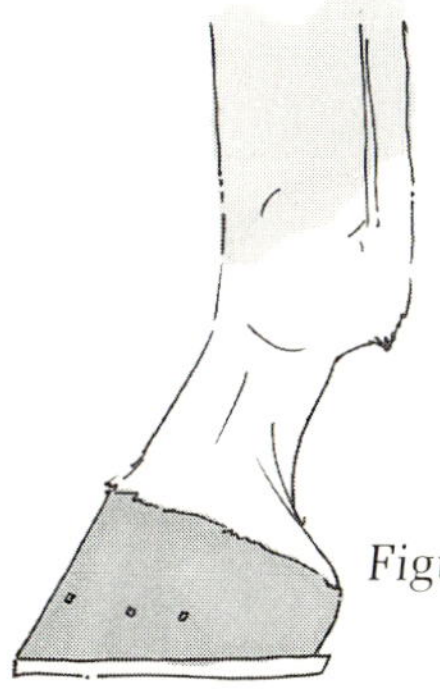

Figure 13.5

SHAPE AND QUALITY OF INDIVIDUAL HOOVES

The horse should have paired hooves of the same angle, the same length and the same shape.

The hind hooves are more ovoid than the fore, and they are approximately five degrees steeper in angle.

White hooves tend to be softer than dark hooves and they

develop cracks more easily. However, they do not differ in size because of the colour disparity.

WEAR PATTERNS

One should take the opportunity to look at a shoe that has been removed from one's horse: it holds invaluable information on how he has worked over the past few weeks. The first thing to look for is the point at which the horse is breaking over: is it to the centre of the toe, or is the horse developing a tendency to break over to the outside?

Secondly, compare the branches of the shoe to see whether both have worn down to the same thickness. If one branch is thinner than the other, it indicates that the horse is putting more mass onto that side of his foot, and the farrier will lower the hoof on that side by the correct degree to cause the opposite side of the foot to bear its required load.

INJURY

If a horse has injured himself and muscle has become wasted, his movement may change as a result. The effect of his movement having changed can be seen in the way the hoof or shoe has worn in the *pairs* of incorrect legs (near fore and off fore or near and off hind) rather than in the laterals (near fore and near hind or off fore and hind).

When a pair of legs is worked unequally, the hoof of the leg doing less work becomes smaller because it bears mass for a shorter period than the hoof doing more work. Conversely the hoof doing more work and therefore taking a greater load tends to become more spread out.

RIDER'S IMPRESSION OF HOW THE HORSE IS GOING

Don't underestimate your instinct. You can often tell a lot merely from the feel you have while on the horse's back. You know your horse; you are aware of his balance and of whether he is favouring one side or leg. Note these impressions, even if you don't fully understand them, and communicate what you feel to the farrier.

Also be aware of the horse in his stable. A farrier working close to the horse's body can pick up by the animal's muscular tension whether he is feeling discomfort in some part of his body. You, or your groom, can develop this awareness, and it is a valuable early-warning system.

USE OF THE FORGE

Every farrier must make use of the forge, whether he works on the forge at home and then takes the prepared shoes with him, or whether he carries a portable forge from yard to yard.

Most horses can be shod from ready-bought shoes, but the alterations needed to ensure perfect fit can only be effected by working the hot shoe in a forge. The forge is also used to prepare special shoes and to draw clips.

Hot shoeing, when the farrier works the shoe in the forge and immediately applies it to the hoof, ensures a perfect fit between foot and shoe, as the precise levelness of the foot can be gauged. A foot that has been shod *hot* tends to hold together well.

Be aware that inexperience with hot shoeing can lead to excessive burning of the hoof. This may happen if the hoof hasn't been trimmed straight, and is made worse if the farrier then attempts to rectify the problem with excess burning of the hoof instead of retrimming it correctly. This procedure is detrimental to the hoof because it causes the hoof to become dry and brittle.

COLD SHOEING

The fitting and nailing of a cold shoe to a hoof should be that of a flat shoe onto a prepared flat hoof. The work necessary on the shoe must have already been done at a forge. It is possible for an experienced farrier to do this if he knows the horse and is familiar with his feet.

TYPES OF SHOES

Standard shoes (for thoroughbreds) are 17 mm to 20 mm broad and 8 mm thick. Showjumpers should be shod with the lightest shoe possible, with due regard to the pressures the shoe will face. Too light a shoe will bend and spread under work and for this reason I do not like to shoe jumpers with polo or training plates.

CORRECTIVE SHOEING

This is achieved by working on the hoof itself; by fitting a normal shoe with changes where necessary; or by making a specific shoe by hand in the forge, a shoe designed to contend with that horse's particular problem.

CLIPS

These are semicircular or triangular tabs of steel drawn from the shoe while it is hot, normally from the toe of the front shoes and the sides of hind shoes (quarter clips). Clips help to secure the shoe to the hoof, especially when the horse lands over a jump or twists on takeoff.

Figure 13.6

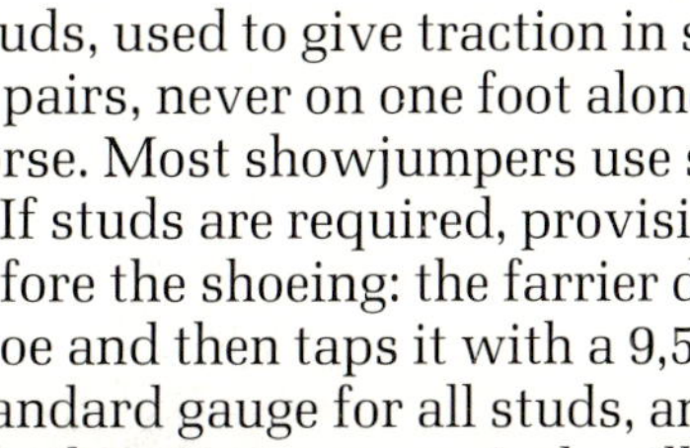

Figure 13.7

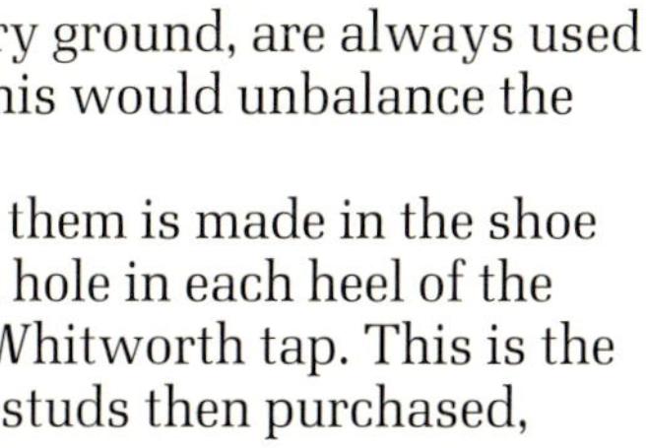

Figure 13.8

STUDS

Studs, used to give traction in slippery ground, are always used in pairs, never on one foot alone, as this would unbalance the horse. Most showjumpers use studs.

If studs are required, provision for them is made in the shoe before the shoeing: the farrier drills a hole in each heel of the shoe and then taps it with a 9,5 mm Whitworth tap. This is the standard gauge for all studs, and the studs then purchased, whether square or conical, will fit.

Studs can be dangerous in certain sports, for instance polocrosse, where the shoe can grip into the ground while the leg twists and cause it to fracture on a sharp turn.

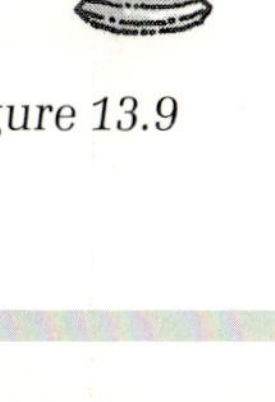

Figure 13.9

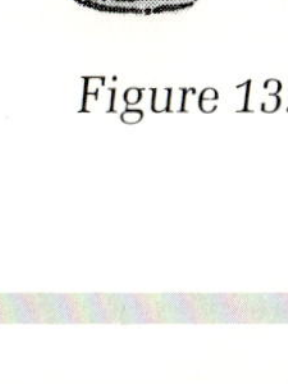

Figure 13.10

Figure 13.11

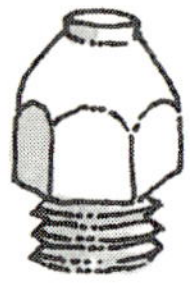

Figure 13.12

The most common use of studs is in the hind shoes only. However, some riders choose to use studs in both hind and front shoes by fitting a stud to each heel, and others choose to use two studs in the heel of each hind shoe, and one stud on the outside of each front shoe.

Large studs are used in wet, soft going, while dry grass requires smaller studs.

Studs should be removed immediately after use because leaving them in means the horse has to cope with walking on a hoof tilted to an unnatural angle, which puts stress on his feet and limbs by causing tendons and ligaments to tighten.

PADS

Certain materials — polypropylene, leather, or plastic compounds — can be shaped and inserted between the hoof and the shoe to protect the sole and frog.

The material most commonly used is 3 mm flat-sheet polypropylene. Leather is no longer in favour as it loses shape when wet, allows seepage of moisture and is generally too thick for the purpose.

The pad can be a rim pad, an ovoid with a hole in the centre or a full pad.

RIM PAD

A rim pad is cut to the same width as the shoe and is used either as a portion or as a whole to add length to the hoof where required.

OVOID PAD

An ovoid pad is used where a horse needs some extra coverage on the sole, usually for protection; the opening allows for circulation of air and for moisture exchange.

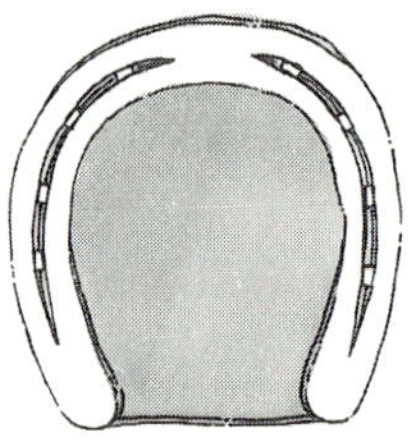

Figure 13.13

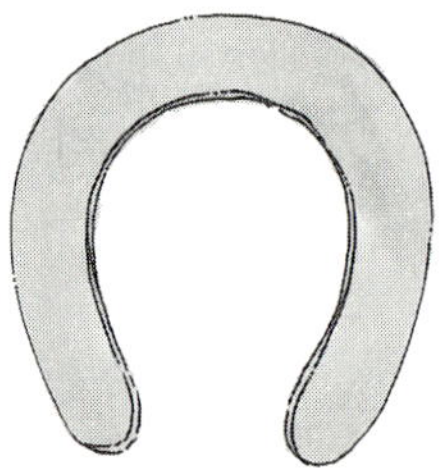

Figure 13.14

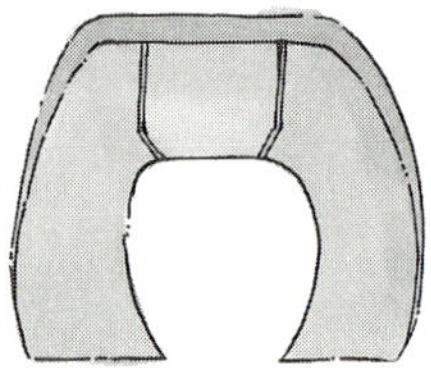

Figure 13.15

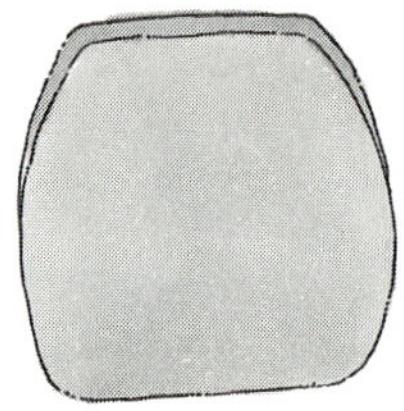

Figure 13.16

FULL PAD

The full pad is cut to the same shape as the underneath of the hoof and is then nailed to the shoe.

When a full pad is used, attention must be paid to the correct packing of the hoof. The pad must totally seal the base of the hoof to prevent dirt or sand accumulating under the pad.

The foot does not suffer from being closed off because it does not breathe.

To ensure that there is no space between foot and pad, pack as follows:

- Liberally apply Stockholm tar to the base of the hoof, then fill the concave area with cotton wool. The cotton wool must be evenly distributed across the sole area to ensure even contact. Spread Stockholm tar on the pad, then nail the pad into position. The Stockholm tar acts as an antiseptic agent and, if the hoof is properly packed in this manner, no thrush will develop in the foot.

- An alternative packing substance is a rubber sealant which, when dry in the foot, is spongy. A disadvantage with this material, however, is that as the hoof grows, the sealant tends to become loose because it is not as adaptable as the viscous Stockholm tar. As a result moisture can seep in.

COMMON PROBLEMS AND CORRECTIVE ACTION

For ease of reference, I have divided common problems into the following categories:

- Movement problems
- Mechanical disorders
- Bone disorders
- Injuries
- Other.

MOVEMENT PROBLEMS

A horse's conformation and level of fitness contribute to his movement or way of going.

A problem relating to the horse's movement or action can in some cases (depending upon the source and severity of the problem) be eased or eradicated by correct trimming and shoeing.

STUMBLING

If a horse does not pick up his feet so that he clears the ground as he moves, he will stumble. This problem is usually associated with the front feet, rather than the hind feet.

CAUSES

- Long toes.
- Tiredness.
- Laziness.
- Imposition of work beyond the horse's level of schooling.
- Classical sign of high suspensory disease (see *Bone Disorders*), neck problems or chips.

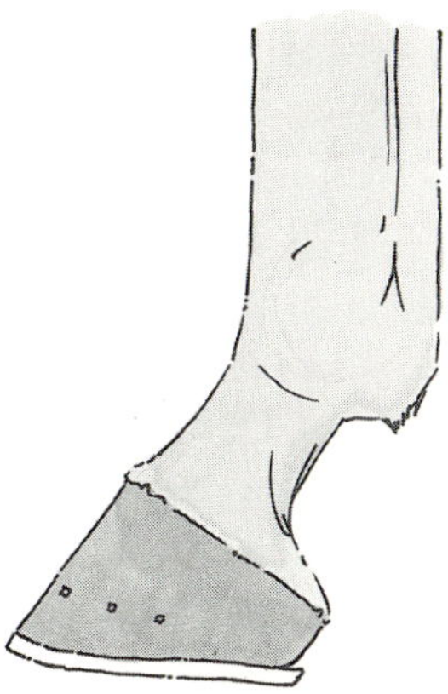

Figure 13.17

ACTION

- If the cause is inadequate training or fitness, rectify accordingly. This applies throughout this section.
- Trim hoof as short as possible.
- Roll the toes of the shoes so that the shoe is rolled upwards between the two toenail holes for the thickness of a shoe, which is 8 mm.
- Consult a vet.

BRUSHING

Brushing occurs when the inside of one hoof strikes the inside of the opposite leg, normally in the area between the coronet and the fetlock. Brushing can occur in front or hind feet, but is more common behind. Horses that toe-out are prone to brushing.

CAUSES

- Conformation — cow-hocked or toed-out horses.
- Incorrect trimming.
- Shoes that protrude at the sides.
- Tiredness.
- Imbalance.
- Lack of fitness.

ACTION

- Observe how the horse moves. Most horses can be helped by lowering the inside of the foot at trimming. Other horses, depending on their action, will benefit from lowering the outside of the foot.
- Set the inside branch of the shoe slightly under, with the edge of the hoof overhanging.
- Leave the outside branch of the shoe longer.

OVERREACHING

An overreach occurs when the toe of a hind foot strikes the tendon or bulb of a foreleg or foot.

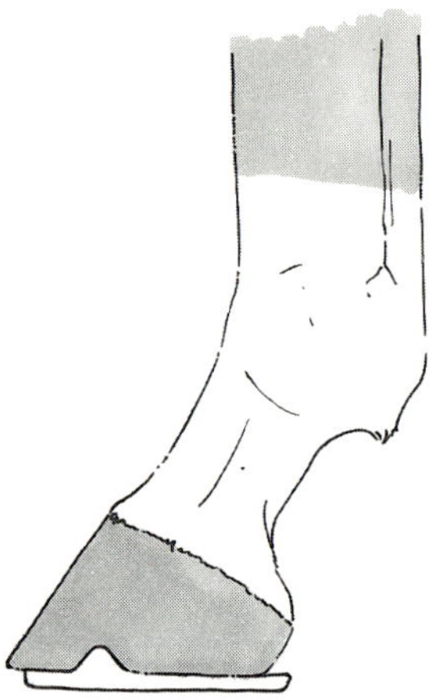

Figure 13.18

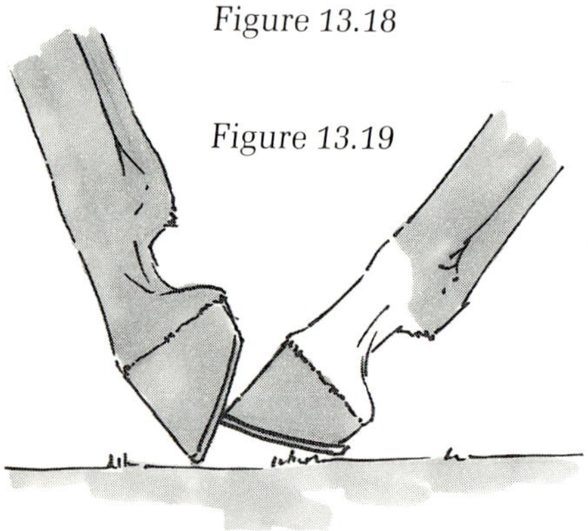

Figure 13.19

CAUSES

- Working powerfully from behind.
- Short back.
- Long legs.
- Angles too low in front.
- Connection on landing (when jumping) is exacerbated when the going is soft, which slows the getaway of the horse's front legs.

ACTION

The intention is to work on the timing of the horse's movement to increase the getaway speed of the front feet. This can be achieved by the following methods:

- Raise the angle of the front hooves.
- Shorten the toes (see Figure 13.17 on previous page).
- Remove flares.
- Shoe with a lighter shoe.
- Roll the toes of the shoes.
- Close-fit the shoes at the heels and taper these heels.

On the hind feet:

- Retain a normal angle.
- Set the shoe under at the toe.
- Extend the heels of the shoes so that they are longer behind — this brings the foot down sooner.
- Round out and smooth the inside border.

FORGING

Forging occurs when the toe of the hind shoe hits the ground surface of the front shoe or the sole of that foot. It is typified by a clicking sound which is heard mainly at the trot, but also at the walk.

Its causes are similar to those of overreaching, but forging will not necessarily develop into overreaching.

ACTION Shoe as for overreaching.

SLOW BREAK-OVER

Observed when the horse is in action.

CAUSES
- Toes too long.
- Angles too low.
- Long sloping pasterns.

ACTION
Shoe as for overreaching.

EXCESSIVE WEARING OF SHOES

Seen in shoes that wear through before the completion of a shoeing cycle.

CAUSES
- Shoes too light.
- Uneven gait.
- Increase in work.
- Tendency to slide the foot as contact is made with the ground.

ACTION
- Correct thickness of shoe, which should not exceed 8 mm to 10 mm.
- Strengthen the shoes by building them up with a hard surface welding rod at the toe and heels.

PULLING OF SHOES

A correctly shod horse will rarely *lose* a shoe in his shoeing cycle, but all horses are capable of pulling shoes off. A horse will usually pull his shoes when he's loose in the paddock, but showjumpers may pull a shoe on landing after a jump.

Figure 13.20

CAUSES
- Front shoes are pulled from behind by the hind foot as the horse is being worked.
- Pawing at a fence can hook and pull a front shoe.
- Hind shoes can be hooked in fences or loosened by continuous kicking against a stable wall or door.
- In summer, irritation by flies can cause a horse to stamp his feet repeatedly. Some horses hit the ground flat, while others make initial contact with the toe. This incessant knocking causes the shoe to shift and come loose.
- Thin, brittle walls (see under *Mechanical Disorders*).

ACTION
- Strong quarter clips, possibly with one extra clip on the outer branch of the shoe, to secure the shoe firmly.
- Larger nails if the hoof is strong enough.
- If shoes are cast because of a horse's kicking, the solution lies not so much in shoeing as in correcting the habit, for kicking *is* a habit and it *can* be corrected. Padding of the stable may help protect the horse's leg from injury due to the concussion, but this does nothing to re-educate the horse. Horses often kick before being fed. Feed kickers first. Incidentally, kicking in the stable can be caused by rats eating at the coronet or oils on the hooves.
- If the shoe is repeatedly pulled during work, the front shoe

must be fitted closely with no extension protruding at the heels.

LANDING TOE FIRST; DIPPING BEHIND

Observed especially behind when, instead of hitting the ground heel first, the foot makes initial contact at the toe. Felt by a rider at its extreme as a dipping motion behind, where the horse's hindquarters appear to collapse momentarily.

CAUSES
- Lameness.
- Angles too low.
- Long toes.

ACTION
- Shorten toes.
- Raise angle with pads if necessary.

DISHING

Motion of a leg that, instead of moving straight, swings either to the inside or the outside.

CAUSES
- Conformation — pigeon-toed horses dish outward; splay-footed horses dish inward.
- Off-set cannon bone.

ACTION
- The primary aim is to bring the break-over point to the centre of the toe.
- For the pigeon-toed horse, shoe wide on the outside of the toe and drop the inside wall — but judiciously, remembering that the horse has to jump on these feet.
- For the splay-footed horse, the opposite applies: shoe wide on the inside of the toe and drop the outside wall.

LOCKING STIFLE

This condition should be referred to a vet. The farrier will help by raising the angles of the hind feet considerably, which often alleviates the condition.

MECHANICAL DISORDERS

Mechanical problems result from the shape of the hoof, uneven growth patterns in the hoof and weak hooves.

CRACKS

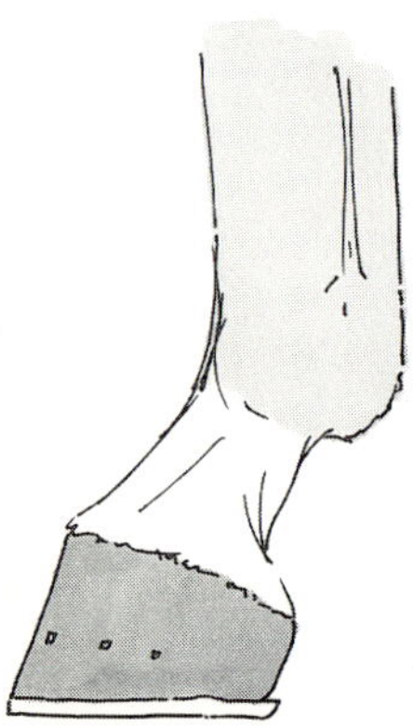

Figure 13.21

Cracks can extend horizontally across the wall from a coronet injury, or they can run vertically from the coronet to the ground. They can also start at ground level and travel up to the coronet. Horizontal cracks tend to occur towards the heels.

CAUSES
- Weakness in hoof.
- Constant rapping of poles when jumping.
- Shoes too short at the heels and therefore giving insufficient support to the foot.

Vertical cracks may occur only in the horny wall or they may

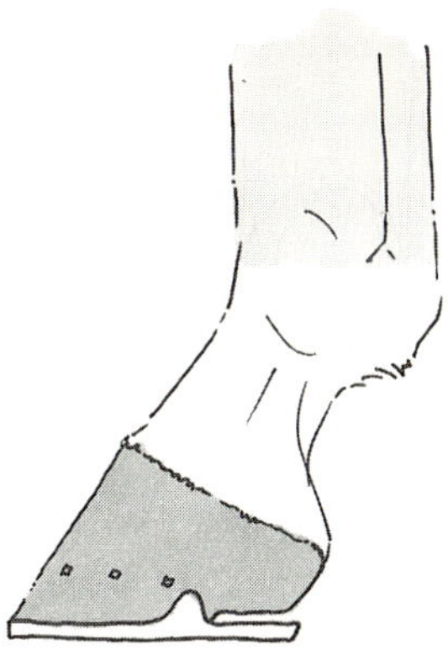

Figure 13.22

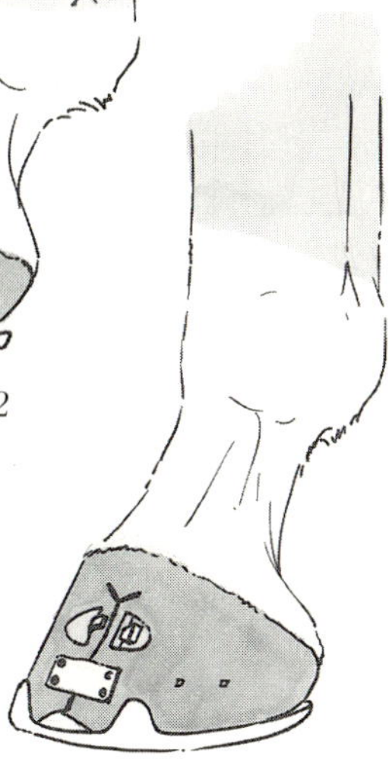

Figure 13.23

extend into the sensitive structures, in which case they may bleed.

CAUSES
- Dry hooves.
- Hoof walls too thin.
- Unbalanced hooves which do not come down flat.
- Injury to coronet.
- Excessively long hooves.
- Excessive concussion, indicated by downward cracks.

ACTION
- Relieve the pressure on the crack by trimming the hoof away at the base of an upward crack. Burn across the top of the crack to prevent extension.
- Infection must first be controlled.
- The crack must be immobilised by:
  - — nailing across the crack;
  - — screwing a plate on;
  - — stitching with wire;
  - — using epoxy and combinations of the above.

HIGH HEELS

The angle of the hoof is more upright than that of the pastern.

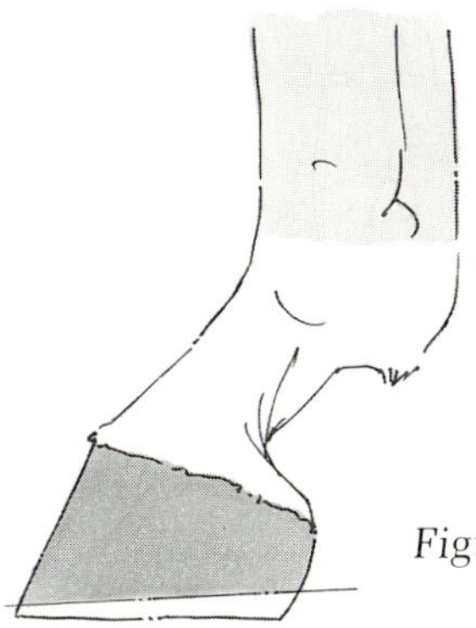

Figure 13.24

CAUSES
- Incorrect trimming.
- Chronic laminitis.
- A natural boxiness that tends towards contraction.

ACTION
- Reduce the heels to bring the angle of the hoof down to that of the pastern. This may have to be done progressively over several shoeings.
- Never trim to an angle lower than that of the pastern. To do so will cause the horse to break down.

LOW HEELS

This occurs when the angle of the pastern is more upright than that of the hoof.

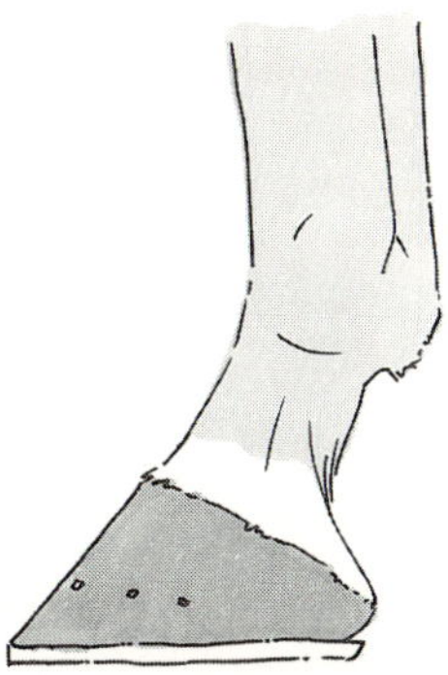

Figure 13.25

CAUSES
- Incorrect trimming.
- Poor conformation.
- Excessive friction between shoe and hoof.

ACTION
- Shoe with a full long shoe, extending well back at heels.
- Bar shoes are recommended in most cases.
- The flatter the hoof, the more the shoe must tend to an egg-bar. In many cases this alone is sufficient to cause the heels to reach their required length.
- In cases where the rate of friction equals the rate of growth, the foot will have to be raised artificially to bring the angle of the hoof in line with the pastern. Wherever possible, I like to use wedge pads for this purpose and I prefer those made of

plastic or aluminium. It is also a good idea to roll the toes of the shoes.

- The combination of bar shoes, rolled toes and wedges should solve the problem.
- I dislike making a shoe thicker at the heels to raise the hoof as the extra mass of the metal interferes with the horse's action.
- I do not recommend calkins: when they are most needed, they sink into the ground.

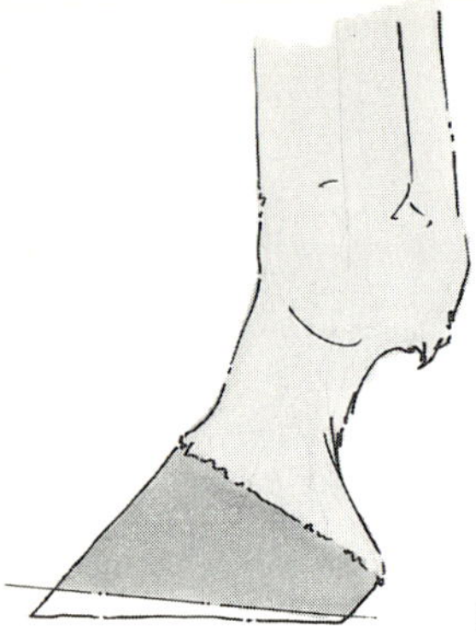

Figure 13.27

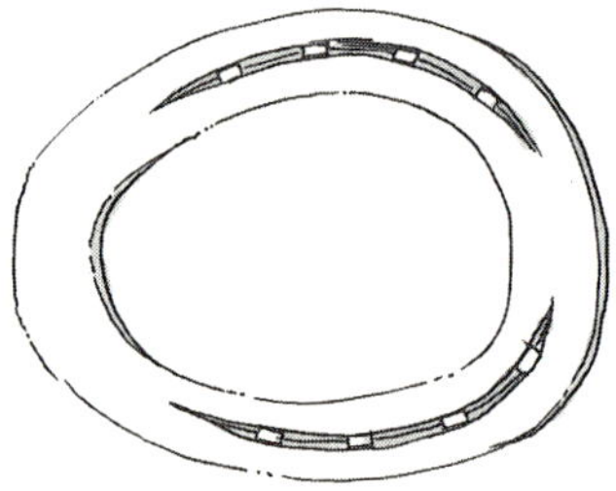

Figure 13.26

SEPARATION

The hoof wall separates from the whiteline, starting at ground level and moving up towards the coronet.

CAUSES

- Weakness in the hoof, possibly following laminitis.
- Excessive moisture.
- Excessive raising of the heels of a horse with low heels. In such a case, separation usually starts at the quarters. (See notes concerning wedges above.)

ACTION

- Clean the site of the separation thoroughly.
- Sear with a hot iron.
- Use side clips if necessary.

SEEDY TOE

This can perhaps best be described as dry rot of the hoof. It is characterised by a cheesy black substance, which increases unless treated, and manifests as a cavity between the hoof wall and the sensitive laminae. The sole may look solid but the hoof sounds hollow in affected areas.

CAUSES

- A blow to the hoof.
- Laminitis in the recovered phase.
- Grit, dirt or sand entering a separation and travelling up the foot.

ACTION

- The farrier must always investigate any dark spots or hollow-sounding areas in the foot.
- All diseased hoof wall must be removed. The diseased area could stretch up to the coronet, but it must be removed regardless. If a thorough job is not done initially, the problem will recur with increasing severity.
- Make a shoe with nail holes to fit the remaining wall.
- A bar shoe is normally effective.
- Use draw clips where necessary.

The hoof soon grows out, providing all the diseased matter was removed.

BRITTLE WALLS

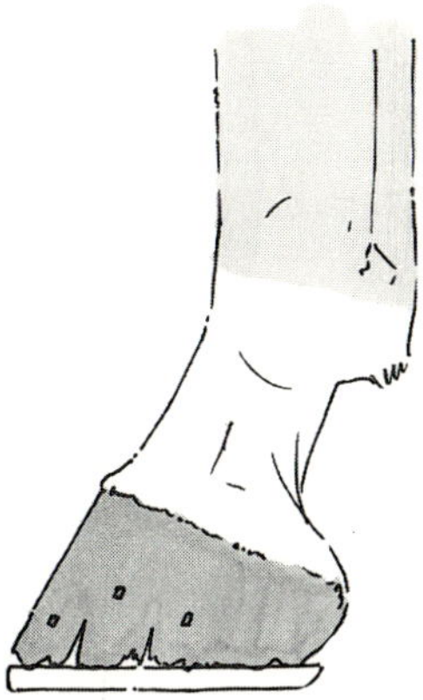

Figure 13.28

This condition is easily perceived as the wall breaks up and shoes are prematurely cast.

CAUSE
Dry hooves — lack of moisture.

ACTION
- Moisturise (see *Extremes of Climate* above).
- Use small high nails.
- Check diet (see *Feeding* above).

CONTRACTED HOOVES

This condition entails feet that have become narrowed through dryness (see *Extremes of Climate*).

CAUSES
- Lack of moisture.
- Incorrect trimming.
- Shoes too tight.

ACTION
- Before anything beneficial can be effected, the hoof must have moisture, specifically water.
- Trim correctly.
- Keep hoof balanced.
- Avoid heel nails.

HOOF-BOUND

Figure 13.29

When a horse becomes hoof-bound, it is usually the result of a bone disorder such as sidebone. The horny hoof wall shrinks because of excessive dryness, and constricts and pinches the sensitive structure within the hoof. The horse will not necessarily go lame, but his movement will be restricted.

CAUSE
Excessive dryness.

ACTION
- It is imperative that the hoof be supplied with moisture.
- Grooving: cut vertical grooves into the hoof wall from just below the coronet to the ground surface. These grooves should be cut as deep as the whiteline; this will relieve pressure on the sensitive structures of the hoof. The hoof's tendency to curl in on itself will also be counteracted. Treated horses show a marked improvement within a few days.

EXCESSIVE FLARING

The walls of the hoof become disproportionately outspread.

CAUSES
- Incorrect trimming, but this condition is also frequently seen in horses that have not been trimmed or shod.
- Chronic laminitis.

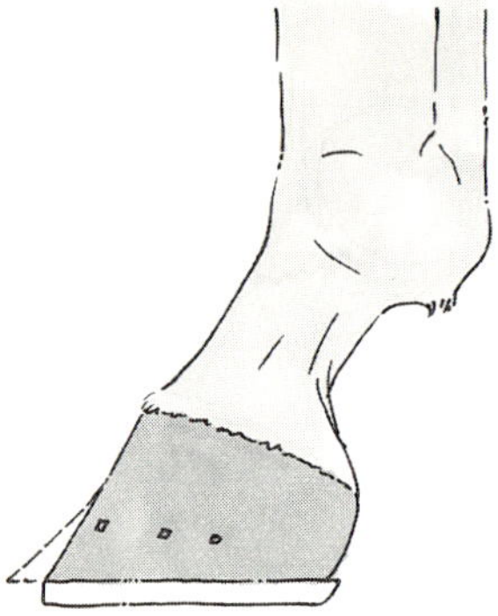

- Unequal application of pressure in the hoof — if the greater degree of pressure is on the inside of the foot, then the outside of that foot may flare.

ACTION

- Remove flares by rasping in a straight line from coronet to ground.
- Balance the hooves.

DIFFERENT RATES OF GROWTH IN A PAIR OF HOOVES

CAUSE

Impaired circulation in one hoof restricts the flow of nutrients to that foot, resulting in slower growth.

ACTION

Trim the hooves to an equal length.

WEAK, FLAT SOLES

Indicated by tendency to bruising and injury.

CAUSES

- Conformation.
- Genetic.
- Laminitis.
- Dropped sole.

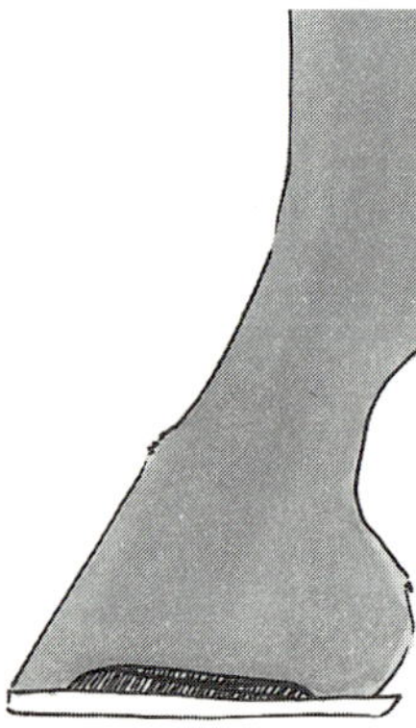

Figure 13.31

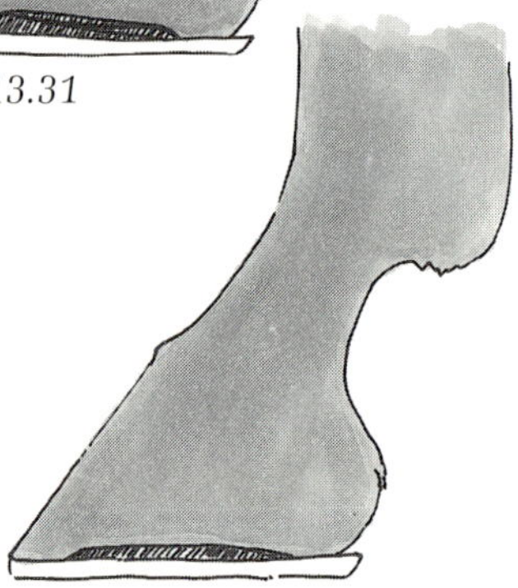

Figure 13.32

ACTION

- During trimming, the sole should not be pared at all.
- Shoe with broad, bevelled shoes — shoes that have been seated out with a hammer so that there is no pressure on the sole when the shoe is nailed on.
- If the horse is bruising badly or going lame, shoe with a full pad.
- Apply a 20 mm flat bar to the shoe a third of the distance from the toe.
- On some horses the use of a hoof hardener (available from a vet) will harden the sole sufficiently to enable the horse to work without pads.

The following conditions should be referred to a vet. I do not attempt a detailed explanation of each disorder, but concentrate instead on the contribution the farrier can make in the correction of the problem.

BONE DISORDERS

RINGBONE

ACTION

- The hoof must be trimmed normally or at a steeper angle, depending on the position of the ringbone and the instructions of the vet. If a hoof is to be trimmed at a steeper angle, this must be done extremely carefully.

- Roll the toe of the shoe.
- Shoe with a pad to absorb concussion.
- In some instances, groove the hoof to relieve pressure.

NAVICULAR

ACTION
- Raise angles of feet, if necessary using wedges.
- Apply a full pad if necessary.
- Bar shoes are frequently advisable.

SPLINTS

ACTION
- Balance foot well.
- Roll the toe of the shoe.
- Shoe with a pad to absorb concussion if necessary.

SIDEBONES

ACTION
- Trim the hoof to the angle at which the horse is happiest.
- Groove the hoof.
- Roll the toe of the shoes.
- Omit heel nails.

INJURIES

BRUISING

This may affect the sole, frog or heel.

CAUSES
- Thinness of the sole.
- Excessive pressure on the sole due to sand packing underneath the hoof.
- The horse having trodden on a sharp stone.

ACTION
- If the horse is lame, poultice the foot.
- Shoe with full pad.

CORNS

Corns result from bruising in a particular area, namely the seat of the corn at the heels.

CAUSES
- Hooves that have been allowed to grow over the shoe.
- Excessive concussion.
- Too small a shoe.
- Dirt between hoof and shoe at the heels.
- Navicular disease.
- Weak heels.
- Low heels.

ACTION
- Corns must be excised.
- Poultice.
- Remove the pressure between the seat of the corn and the shoe.
- Shoe with bevelled shoes.
- Shoe with egg-bar shoes.
- Shoe with a full pad to alleviate concussion.

OTHER PROBLEMS

LAMINITIS

Inflammation of the laminae can affect all four feet or only the front hooves. The hooves are tender and the soles can become flattened.

ACTION

- It is imperative that this condition be treated in consultation with a vet.
- Rotation of the pedal bone may have occurred, and X-rays should be taken to determine the exact position of this bone.
- Trim only if the X-rays show this to be necessary. Shoeing for acute laminitis is different to shoeing for chronic, recovering or recovered laminitis.
- There is often a bulge of dead hoof at the toe and this must be removed.
- A reversed shoe is effective as a bar shoe with no pressure in front.

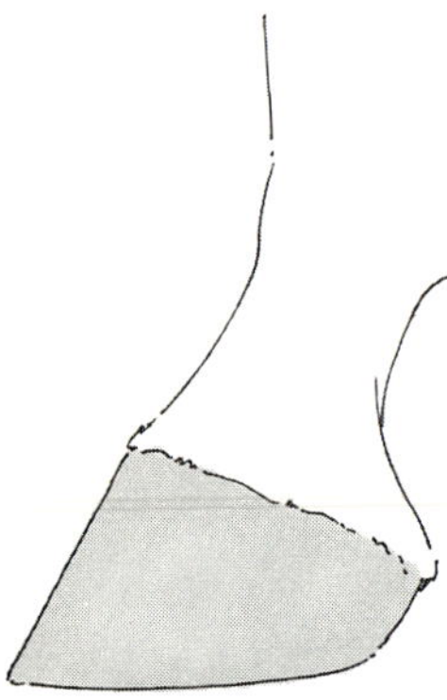

Figure 13.33

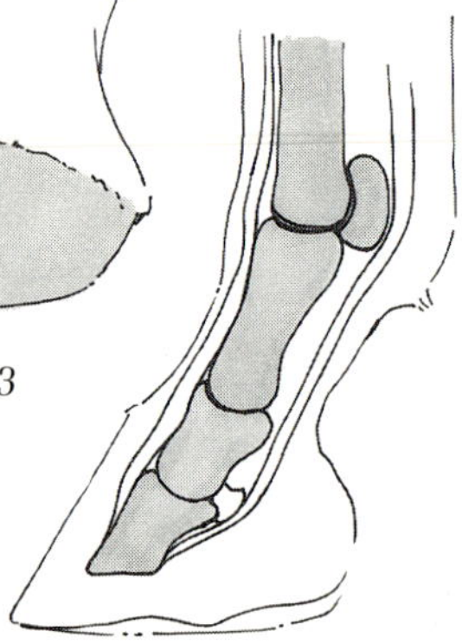

Figure 13.34

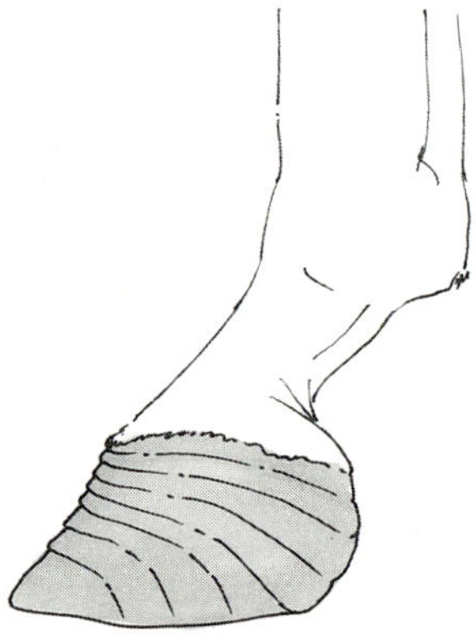

Figure 13.35

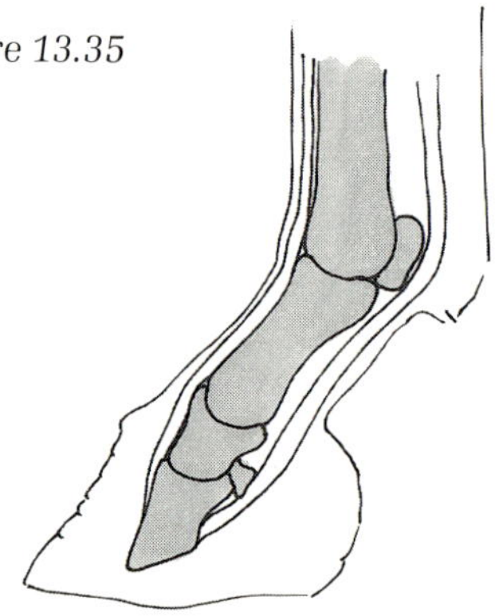

Figure 13.36

- A full bar shoe may be fitted.
- Alternatively, a shoe with a bar a third of the way down the web may be used (see *Weak, Flat Soles*).
- Sometimes pads are necessary, but it is important not to overcorrect rotation because the tendons have contracted.

THRUSH

Thrush is a necrotic condition of the clefts of the frog characterised by a foul odour. This can extend into the sensitive structures.

ACTION

- All diseased tissue must be removed, regardless of how deep it has penetrated.
- Wash the hoof with disinfectant.
- Apply a drying agent: copper sulphate, gentian violet, hydrogen peroxide and domestic bleach are all effective. I do not like formalin as it tends to burn the horse.
- Poultice if necessary.
- Change the bedding.

14

Feeding the Showjumper

I HAVEN'T gone into detail with regard to feeding the showjumper because there are so many publications dedicated to the art of feeding, I felt there was no point. I have therefore settled for explaining my basic routine but I hope you will bear in mind that what suits me and my horses may not suit you and yours.

I give a great deal of thought to how my horses are fed because I ask a lot of them and they can't supply it if I don't ensure that they've got the physical reserve to do so. I'm not just talking about making sure they've got the energy to jump round an A Grade course; I'm talking about the general good health and wellbeing that come from feeding each horse sensibly and in accordance with his needs.

Most riders accept that there are standard feeding rules, such as that a horse should have a constant supply of clean fresh water, that he should always be offered water *before* he is fed (particularly if water is not readily available to him at all times), that only clean, good quality food should be fed; and that a horse should be fed in accordance with age, temperament and the work being done. However, despite the fact that most horseowners accept these rules, it's all too common to see them being broken, particularly the one relating to feeding in accordance with age, temperament and the work being done. Too many horseowners think they are feeding their horse correctly simply because they are giving him two or maybe three feeds a day of good quality food plus good hay and fresh water, but what they haven't done, is assess what the horse actually needs — they should do this and then ensure that the diet offered fulfils those needs.

Assessing what your horse needs isn't difficult, but it requires careful thought. If you don't obey this rule, your horse won't perform to the best of his ability and if he's denied what he needs for any length of time, there is a risk that his health may break down.

One thing I may do a little differently to most people is feed concentrates only twice (morning and night) rather than three time a day; I find that my horses do very well on this routine. However, my horses have hay *ad lib:* they are never without a net of hay to pick at. If I check the yard at night and find that a horse has finished his net, I give him more. I also feed hay in the paddock because there isn't any good grazing to speak of in the Transvaal and my horses have a constant supply of clean fresh water at all times.

It wouldn't be practical for me to explain precisely what I feed each individual horse in my stable, but as a general rule, I do the following for most horses: horses in work receive one or two double handfuls of cut lucerne per meal. I cut the lucerne myself but it is possible to buy it in bags, ready-cut.

Horses receiving cut lucerne are usually fed whatever quantity of Epol Rider Cubes I feel they need to enable them to perform and maintain condition.

I feed rolled oats to horses that are slightly lazy and I sometimes supplement a horse's diet with oats while he's competing.

I also feed Emol (a molasses meal) and, of course, a handful of coarse salt.

I keep digestive bran handy and use it for a weekly bran mash, and on that note, I'd like to add that if a horse has an infection or strain of any kind, his food should be cut so that he is only receiving a little lucerne, bran, salt, Emol, and as much teff as he can eat. (N.B. If a horse is out of action for some time his shoes should be removed. Put down thick clean bedding for him: it will do him no good whatsoever to stand on cement for 10 or 12 hours of the day if confined to the box.)

If my competition horses tend to get a bit fat on just the Rider Cubes I often use either two-thirds Rider Cubes to a third Competition Cubes, half and half or, depending on the horse, just Competition Cubes. I once had quite a lazy horse and I tried the Epol Gold Cup Racehorse Cubes on him, but even that didn't do the trick so I ended up feeding him a mixture called Epol Triple Crown. This worked very well and kept him full of himself. I have one who does very well on Millard Race Horse Cubes.

I don't believe in feeding a lot of extras unless it appears to be absolutely necessary as cubes form a balanced ration.

When feeding bran or oats, I sprinkle more water on the food than I would if I were feeding cubes: I'm very careful about wetting cubes because they may swell and cause a blockage.

I think that it is most important to mix the food properly and I lay each individual feed out on a large piece of sacking before sprinkling it lightly with water and thoroughly mixing it. I mix it on sacking rather than in a bucket because I find it far more efficient to do it in this way, and I take care to clean or change the sacking regularly so that it doesn't become sour from old food.

On that note, I'd like to add that it is also most important to keep the mangers scrupulously clean: a good scrub with salt and water and a thorough drying every now and again is a good idea.

Remember to keep a check on the horse's teeth: you can feed a horse the most appropriate diet in the world but if he can't chew it, he won't be able to digest it properly. Also see that he is dewormed regularly.

I hope this gives you a basic outline of how I keep my horses in top condition: feeding is an art, but it's an art anybody can learn.

15

TRAVELLING THE HORSE

WHETHER you are travelling your horse a short or long distance, the following guidelines will help to ensure that he arrives safely and in a frame of mind conducive to competing:

- Try to feed at least one hour before loading the horse for a short trip and two hours before a long trip. This isn't always possible, but it *is* the ideal. To do otherwise can result in colic as excitement can prevent a horse from digesting his food properly.
- Going to local shows you may or may not wish to plait your horse up before loading him. I prefer to have my horses ready before travelling them, and I try to make sure they can't rub their plaits out en route.
- Bandage the horse sensibly: this means using good thick cotton wool or bandage pads under the bandages. Don't bandage too tightly. I don't use hock or knee protectors as I find that they often irritate the horse, but when bandaging I bandage from below the knee well down over the fetlock joint to the coronet.
- Use a poll guard. It might save your horse's life one day.
- You, and only you, should put on your horse's tail bandage. *Never* leave it to a groom, because if a tail bandage is put on too tightly (which is all too easy to do) your horse may lose his tail as a result. If a tail receives a poor blood supply for as short a time as 20 minutes a problem may develop which could result in the vet having to amputate the tail bones. If you are travelling a long distance, it's a wise precaution to do without a tail bandage altogether. If the horse has a tendency to rub his tail when travelling, give him more room or travel him diagonally; or put up with it — his tail hairs will grow back but his tail bones won't.
- Feed. Take whatever feed you will need for each horse during the show.
- Water. I offer my horses a drink before loading them. Once I get to the show, I use only tap water. Never let your horse drink from a communal trough: it's just asking for him to get whatever nasty little virus is doing the rounds.
- Hay. As a rule, I put up a net on the way to the show (especially if the show is seven or eight hours away) because

it gives the horse something to pick at, which settles him down.

- I put the following items on the lorry:
  - Show bridle for each horse fully fitted with whatever bit, noseband and martingale he uses in the ring.
  - Saddles with stirrup leathers and irons, girth, circingle and numnah attached.
  - Several pairs of tendon boots for the front legs, small back boots for behind and, of course, overreach boots. Don't forget studs and stud spanners.
  - Running reins and whip.
  - I always make sure I have a spare bridle fully fitted and a spare girth and circingle, as well as several different types of bit in case I need one of them.
  - I have a special compartment for rugs and blankets. As I am sponsored, I travel with six night rugs, six day sheets, six sweat sheets and six saddle-cloths, all of course bearing the sponsor's name and logo. I also keep several waterproof sheets handy.
  - Then there are the machines that always travel with me: magneto pulse, feradic and ultrasound.
  - I take the following veterinary products: a thermometer, antiseptic fluid, wound spray and powder, poulticing, bandages, cotton wool and tape, scissors, electrolyte powders, Epsom salts, bicarbonate of soda, penicillin or any vitamin injections I might need. (Bear in mind that horses have been known to die as a result of receiving certain injections: check with your vet first. I also take drenches in case of colic, needles and syringes. Do not inject a horse intravenously or drench a horse yourself — leave that to a vet.
  - Grooming equipment: hoof oil, grooming brushes and elastic bands for plaiting (I don't use thread and needles).
  - Yard equipment: brooms, forks, buckets, feed, scoop, and the feed bags I use for laying out the feed.
  - For myself I pack boots, boot polish, boot pullers, boot jack, breeches, long socks and knee-high stockings, American shirts and collars, tie pin, hard hat, hair net, jacket and clothes brush, spurs, gloves and crop.

LOADING

- Once all the equipment is in the lorry, I load the horses. This is where the first of a number of accidents can happen if you're not careful. Accidents can't always be avoided, of course, but the chance of your horse having one can be greatly reduced if you give a little thought to loading up.
- The first accident can occur before the horse even gets into the box. If the trailer is at the side of the road and the horse suddenly jumps off the ramp or runs backwards and swings into the road, he can cut or bruise himself, squash the handler or be hit by a car. Therefore, position the trailer in as safe a place as the circumstances allow.

- If a horse falls off a ramp, he can easily cut a leg or injure a tendon. Good bandaging can make the difference between a bad cut and a slight graze. When a horse is being unloaded, he can just as easily fall off the ramp. Ramp gates will help avoid this problem.
- If you are using a trailer, always put the breaching across before you tie the horse, and never attempt to put up the ramp until the breaching is across.
- A horse that panics when tied is likely to compound the problem by rearing, possibly hitting his poll (which should have a poll guard on it) or getting his front legs over the breast bar.
- Many horses become claustrophobic if they have a solid partition to the floor on each side of them, especially if they can't spread their hind feet well apart. This may cause a horse to panic, and it is therefore sometimes safer to travel two horses side by side without a partition, providing neither horse is likely to kick the other. I never use a partition in a two horse box.
- The most common injury sustained by horses travelling in a horsebox or trailer results from the horse suddenly going beserk. A horse can then injure anything because he throws himself around. If the box is padded, the horse usually suffers only minor injuries, but if the horse is in a very basic trailer he can cut himself to such an extent that he may have to be destroyed.
- One of the most serious and lethal injuries horses sustain when travelling is due to their feet going through the floor. Urine rots wood and steel, so it is essential that the floor of a horsebox be regularly checked.
- If a horse has been involved in an accident and appears to be bleeding profusely, don't panic. A horse can lose a lot of blood before he is in any danger of bleeding to death. Take a second or two to assess the situation and see whether it is as serious as you think. Apply a pressure bandage until a vet arrives. Try to keep the horse warm and calm.
- One of the worst places for bleeding is when a horse cuts himself about the coronet. Bind a bandage around the coronet.
- Horses can get travel sickness, a form of anaerobic bacterial pneumonia. The reason why people drench a horse with vitamins and electrolytes, prior to travelling a long distance, is to avoid a buildup of toxic bacteria in the gut. I also inject with long-acting penicillin.

AIR TRAVEL

- Horses are travelled in crates, and the size, make and shape of the crates are vital to the safety and comfort of the horse. A crate must be high enough to prevent a horse from jumping out and from getting his front legs over the side. A crate must also be light and strong, especially if it doesn't have a roof. Some airlines have their own crates with roofs and some have straps to hold the horses in. The strap is designed to keep the horse in the crate should the plane hit an air pocket or vacuum, but straps can sometimes cause a horse to panic.

- Horses in planes are better off without bandages and they should have their shoes removed so that they can get a good grip on the rubber matting that covers the bottom of the crate.
- A horse is secured into the crate by an adjustable cow collar. Under normal circumstances, the rule is that a horse should never be tied by something unbreakable. Travelling a horse by air is the exception to that rule: it is simply too dangerous to allow the possibility of a horse breaking free and risking the lives of all on board as a result. This is why horses are destroyed if they manage to smash their way out of the crate or if by chance they escape from the crate in a panic.
- It is crucial that the horse travels in the same direction as the plane is flying, otherwise he will lose his balance and fall over. Left to their own devices, the majority of airlines prefer to travel horses sideways because in this way they can travel three to a pallet — insist that this isn't done with your horse.
- If a horse needs a tranquilliser, make sure the vet uses one suitable for a horse being travelled by air. It's no good giving a horse something that is going to knock him off his feet, because it is essential for him to retain his balance at all times.
- If a horse is panicking when travelling the vet should ideally get a tranquilliser into the horse, preferably intravenously, although this is rarely possible in such circumstances. In this situation, use a twitch on the ear because this is more effective than a twitch on the nose.
- If a horse panics, blindfold him.
- A handler must accompany the horse, and that handler must be experienced. *Don't* send a novice.
- If a horse has to be put down, the vet will use a captive bolt.

Some horses are perfect travellers by air. If so, it's better for them to travel by air than by road (or in the case of a horse travelling to another continent, by sea). They'll arrive in a fraction of the time and with half the stress of a horse travelling in a box.

16

A Brief Word about Riding

Bronwyn Redwin, a junior A Grade pupil

THIS book is largly concerned with training and caring for the showjumper, but it wouldn't be complete without a few words devoted to the rider.

All riders need a trainer; somebody competent to teach them how to ride correctly and ensure that no bad habits creep in over the years.

I have always enjoyed teaching and I feel that it is important to be able to help others by imparting to them what one has learnt over the years. It is very rewarding to see riders improving and starting to do well in competitions. I don't teach beginners who are learning to ride and jump and I don't supply horses or ponies for my pupils. My pupils come to me with their horses. The only time I go out to teach is when I have courses running in other venues. When I run courses I usually teach from CD, JD and D grade upwards, although in the last year or so I have cut down and now only teach the higher levels.

I think it is terribly important that a rider who decides to showjump must really want to do it. It's no use doing it just because your best friend does it or because your parents would like you to do it or because it happens to be the in-thing at the time. To be really good, you have to be truly dedicated and you have to be prepared to work very hard. You also have to be prepared to have patience. To reach the top as a showjumper, your heart has to be in the right place; I will never forget the internationally reknowned German rider Hans Winkler telling a pupil of mine "Put your heart over the jump or give up showjumping". In other words, you must be one hundred percent confident in what you are doing.

Showjumping is a difficult sport because you are not just relying on your own ability, you are relying on the horse's ability as well as the partnership between you and that particular horse. Some of the qualities I would look for in a rider of a junior C or B Grade horse are confidence and temperament. Without a good temperament it is very hard to reach the top in any sport. When the chips are down you have to be ice cool, but at the same time, you must have that absolute will to win. Then of course a good eye, concentration and dedication are also very important in the making of a top showjumper.

I am a great believer in correct and good style. For many

A light seat

Three or four strides before take-off

people there is nothing worse than watching a clumsy ballet dancer, for me there is nothing worse than watching an untidy, clumsy showjumping round. If the rider does not have reasonably good style then how can the horse have good style. Although there are exceptions to the rule, I would say that at least 90 per cent of the top showjumping riders in the world are basically correct in their style of riding. I remember my mother once telling me to put a satchel full of books on my back and run along with it loose and flapping to see how unbalanced it felt. Then she said to strap it down onto my back so that it was tight and fitting and then to run so that I could see how much more comfortable it was.

A really good rider can win with minimum effort. Remember, you are just as fast against the clock with a tight firm strong seat and leg as with your legs kicking and your arms flapping. I always think that the first sign of a nervous rider is when he pushes his hands forward up the horse's neck a stride or two before take-off and then freezes in the saddle or when, having lost confidence, he starts to kick and flap into the fences.

Without a good eye and a good sense of stride and rhythm it is impossible to really succeed. This comes naturally to some riders; I cannot remember ever having battled to see my stride right. However with a good instructor behind you and with a lot of hard work, dedication and confidence you can develop a good eye. When you are not confident, your eye is not one hundred percent. I believe that most top sportsmen, whatever their sport, have never found their sport difficult but have worked very hard to perfect it.

To me showjumping is a great leveller; one minute you can be at the top and winning everything but the next minute you could be sitting on the grand stand and not even competing. You have to be able to take the ups and downs. You may be at the top and then have your horse go lame or become sick and find yourself right out of the major competitions. The equestrian sport is a good character builder!

When a rider first comes to me for lessons there are several points which I concentrate on, including an independent seat, good hands and a nice soft elbow. It is important that a rider has a deep seat, I like to see a rider riding on the flat with the stirrups at least two or three holes longer than for showjumping. He must have a deep heel, his leg must be in the correct position, he must have a straight back but a relaxed hip and most importantly, he must ride proud. When jumping if the rider pulls up his stirrups he will automatically have a lighter seat, but it is important to remember that a lighter seat is not a standing seat, the lower legs must always be underneath you and not stuck out in front of you.

On approach to the jump I like the rider to ride with a light seat and the body at about a 45 degree angle. The rider should keep a light contact on his horse's mouth and sink lightly down into the saddle three or four strides before the jump, close leg on takeoff, drive his horse's hindlegs underneath him and lighten the forehand. If he lets his rein loop as the horse is midway over the jump, he will lose contact with his horse's mouth and the horse may start to lose confidence and hang back a little over his jump. In other words, he may not travel forward as he would on a very light elastic type of contact.

Please don't misunderstand me here: I am not saying for one minute that a rider should hold the horse's head or hang onto his mouth as he goes over the jump; all I'm saying is that the weight of the rein should be there between his mouth and the rider's hand.

As the horse is going over the jump, the rider's seat and body should follow his rhythm. The rider shouldn't be ahead of the jump — in other words leaning forward and up the horse's neck when he's in mid-air. Nor should he have fallen back against the jump (in other words, he shouldn't be "left behind"). If a rider has good balance and a strong leg position with a supple hip, he will find that his mid-air position over the jump will be in rhythm with the horse.

Then, as the horse is landing, the rider's body angle should open up away from the horse's neck; his elbow should open up and his body should move away from his hand. If all this happens correctly, he will land in the correct position and be in balance for his first stride.

I never take for granted that I am a good rider with good style. I work on this every time that I ride or jump because I feel that as I get older, if I do not maintain the style in which I jumped when I was younger, I will only go one way: that is down hill.

It is very easy to pick up bad habits at home, especially when you are working young horses. That is why you should, if possible, always have somebody to watch you, no matter how good you are. I always have my head groom Simon in the paddock when I am jumping, even though he is not a showjumper. To have somebody experienced in the paddock who can correct me is even better: one is never too old to learn! When teaching, I prefer to give private lessons because one can do so much more with the horse and rider in the hour that one has to work with them, but I never restrict myself to an hour when teaching which is probably why I find that my days are never long enough. I have to do group lessons as well but I try never to take more than four or at most five riders together. When I am running a course, I do tend to have more riders, but then I leave myself at least two hours per group and restrict the group to eight riders.

I believe that when teaching one is not only teaching showjumping, I like my riders to ride under my instruction for at least thirty minutes on the flat. During the flat work I make them do a lot of sitting trot, particularly without stirrups. I concentrate on style, on a deep seat, on teaching them the aids, on getting the horses between hand and leg and going forward onto the bridle and on suppling the horses. We do a fair amount of leg yield, shoulder-in, travers, changes of rein, and flying changes with the more advanced horses and riders.

Once a month I try to hold a special equitation lesson for my riders who are interested. We try to cover as much as possible, doing tests and practising the movements one is asked for in equitation. This also means that we do quite a lot of jumping without stirrups and with the reins held in one hand.

In a normal lesson, once the pupils are finished with the flat work, they put their stirrups up two or three holes before we start to jump. The jumping work I do with my pupils is very much the same as what I do with my own horses. For example we may start off with trotting poles to a vertical and once the horses and riders have warmed up reasonably well we continue into a vertical six strides further on. I eventually change the vertical jump into a spread and use the exercise to teach horses and riders to trot quietly over the trotting poles followed by the pop stride over the vertical and a short seven or eight strides into the next vertical keeping their horses on a straight line. Riders learn to shorten the horse's stride by squeezing with their legs and closing the contact of the hand against the mouth. Once we have achieved this, I ask the riders to do the same exercise into the vertical and immediately upon landing to squeeze on with a strong driving leg and seat into six strides to the vertical without losing the contact with their horses' mouths and so not dropping them onto the forehand. It is quite difficult to do this exercise because the horse has got used to the short bouncy stride and then you ask for a longer stronger stride. Once I am satisfied with their progress over the vertical we jump it as a spread. Then we will work at the canter over a single vertical followed by a spread on the circle in both directions. After this both horse and rider should be ready for dog's leg lines, serpentine work over fences, doubles and treble combination work.

All these exercises teach my riders to think, to keep their horses balanced, to ride on a good rhythm, to be controlled and most importantly to see a reasonably good stride. I try to change the course of jumps in the paddock at least once or twice a month so that the exercises are not always the same. I do not believe in overfacing either horse or rider, I don't overbuild the height of the jumps and never build higher than the grade that they are in or that the horses are capable of competing in.

I do not school or work my pupils' horses. I believe that they must learn under my instruction how to school and jump their horses and how to correct their horses' faults. They must learn to follow my instruction and train their horses correctly, so that they will ultimately be able to correct and teach a horse on their own.

I believe that children should start riding a real riding school pony and only once they have learnt balance and to stop the typical kicking and pulling of that sort of pony is it time to progress to dressage and jumping. Then a young rider needs a reasonably well trained pony that will help him learn. To be a successful showjumper, no matter how talented you are, you need the right horse. Many successful juniors with good jumpers bring the same horse through the grades with them and go on to become successful in the adult grades. Unfortunately showjumping is a very expensive sport — juniors should be very grateful to their parents who sponsor them.

There is an old saying, "It takes two lifetimes to learn to ride a horse", and I've come to the conclusion that it's true. I've been riding for over 40 years now, 30 of them at top level, and I learn something new every day. What I've written about riding is a mere drop in the ocean of what there is to know but I hope it will give some indication of the line I like to see a rider take.